K-8

D0475173

60108

CHRISTMAS
ALL AROUND
THE HOUSE

CHRISTMAS ALL AROUND THE HOUSE

Traditional Decorations You Can Make

Florence H. Pettit
Drawings by Wendy Watson

Thomas Y. Crowell Company   New York

Manufactured in the United States of America

Library of Congress Cataloging in Publication Data
Pettit, Florence Harvey.
  Christmas all around the house.
  Bibliography: p.
  Includes index.
  SUMMARY: Instructions for making a variety of Christmas decorations, crafts, and foods that originated in different parts of the world.
  1. Christmas decorations—Juv. lit. [1. Christmas decorations. 2. Handicraft] I. Watson, Wendy. II. Title.
TT900.C4P45   745.59′41   75-37876
ISBN 0-690-01013-3
1 2 3 4 5 6 7 8 9 10

To Jean, who loved Christmas

Other Books by Florence H. Pettit

America's Indigo Blues: Resist-Printed and Dyed Textiles of the Eighteenth Century

America's Printed and Painted Fabrics, 1600-1900

Block Printing on Fabrics

How to Make Whirligigs and Whimmy Diddles and Other American Folkcraft Objects

ACKNOWLEDGMENTS

For their interest and assistance the author gives her sincere thanks to Robert M. Pettit, a patient photographer; to Yvonne Forbath and Gertrude Rys, who remembered *Krampus* from their girlhood days in Vienna; to Margarita Stuard, indefatigable guide to the wonders of Lima and Cuzco; and to Marjorie Krieg and June Henneberger of the United Nations Headquarters Gift Center in New York City.

The author found the following books invaluable and recommends them to anyone who is interested in learning more about Christmas customs: *Christmas the World Over* by Daniel J. Foley, *One Thousand and One Christmas Facts and Fancies* by Alfred Carl Hottes, *The Book of Religious Holidays and Celebrations* by Marguerite Ickis, and *Christmas Customs Around the World* by Herbert H. Wernecke.

CONTENTS

PREFACE

The idea of Christmas as a time of goodwill has endured throughout many centuries, ever since early Christians began to celebrate the birth of Christ. However, there are varied legends and symbols of Christmas and many different ways in which people around the world commemorate the winter holy days.

The traditions of Christmas are meaningful as well as charming, and many are filled with beauty and a sense of wonderment. In some countries certain Christmas customs are more concerned with good omens for the New Year than with strictly religious aspects of the season. But however Christmas is celebrated and whatever its ornaments and activities may be, it is a joyful time that brings universal renewal of the human spirit for the year to come.

In recent times more and more people have begun to enjoy the idea of celebrating Christmas in traditional ways. They are discovering the pleasures of decorating their homes with handmade ornaments made from simple natural materials, and they enjoy doing their own cooking and baking. The whole family joins in the preparations, which gives everyone a sense of participation in the holidays.

In this book we hope to restore to reality some of the traditional ways of celebrating Christmas. Here is a group of decorations that you can make by hand. Some will be familiar to you, and some are known best in the lands where they originated. All of them represent the graceful idea of a hospitable and happy holiday season. These ornaments and decorations are presented as gifts to those who revere the meaning of Christmas, as well as to all who love its festive cheer.

1
A GERMAN
ADVENT WREATH

A glowing anticipation of Christmas

In the Christian calendar Advent is the period that begins on the first Sunday in December and lasts until Christmas. These weeks have for centuries been observed as a time of fasting and prayer, preceding the joyous celebration of the birth of Christ.

Even in families that do not observe the religious solemnity of Advent, everyone feels a decided stirring of excitement as Christmas draws near. It is a time of preparation and anticipation, a time when people feel that good things are about to happen.

There is a simple and lovely symbol of this happy season that has solemn meaning as well as a bright and cheerful glow. It is an evergreen wreath with four red candles encircled in it, one candle representing each Sunday of Advent.

The first wreath of this kind was probably made in Germany—a country where many ideas for the celebration of a Merry Christmas appear to have originated. There it became the custom to

I

The finished Advent wreath,
made by the author

light one candle in the wreath to burn awhile on each successive Sunday evening during Advent until finally on Christmas Eve all four candles were alight. While the candles burned, prayers and verses were said, and families and neighbors joined together in singing hymns.

A century ago in England, the Advent wreath was an elaborate ribbon-trimmed construction of holly and laurel leaves, which hung from the ceiling so that the candlelight shone down from overhead during the singing of carols. A simpler table wreath made of evergreen sprigs with four red candles is more common today and is a meaningful way to mark the anticipation of Christmas.

You can make this handsome holiday wreath from evergreen boughs, adding, if you like, sprigs of boxwood, privet, laurel, holly, or mistletoe. These materials or bits of similar shrubs and greens that grow where you live are easy to find. Making the wreath is so simple that even a beginner can put it together. You can use the same kind of base you need for the Advent wreath to make table wreaths of pine cones, dried seedpods, and nuts. Or you can fashion delightful miniature wreaths to put at each person's place at a festive dinner table. In this season of goodwill, you will find that the *will* is all you really need in order to create these simple but lovely Christmas decorations.

Materials and Tools for the Advent Wreath

SPRIGS OF EVERGREENS, such as hemlock, spruce, white pine, fir, juniper, or arbor vitae. To these, you can add box, privet, pine cones, laurel, holly, or mistletoe.

CANDLES. You will need four bright red ones, 10 inches tall.

CORRUGATED CARDBOARD. You will need three sturdy, flat pieces, each 11 inches square.

RULER, metal-edged, or a steel straightedge

PENCIL

UTILITY KNIFE, heavy handled with a new blade

WOODEN BOARD or sheet of heavy cardboard, to protect your working surface

RUBBER CEMENT with brush attached to lid of container

WHITE PAPER, heavy piece, 11 inches square

PENCIL COMPASS

SCISSORS, sharp-pointed

MASKING TAPE, $3/4$ inch wide

CARDBOARD, shirtboard or similar weight. You will need a piece 4 by 8 inches.

POSTER PAINT, green

PAINTBRUSH, No. 3 or No. 4

AWL or ice pick

PRUNING SHEARS

FLORIST'S WIRE, No. 30

WIRE-CUTTING PLIERS or nippers

FELT. You will need a piece of green or brown felt, 11 inches square, or a piece of green or brown heavy cotton cloth of the same size.

Making the Base of the Wreath

Since the wreath is to be used flat on a table and will be fairly lightweight, it can be constructed over a simple cutout form made of three layers of corrugated cardboard cemented or laminated together. Use the kind of tan-colored cardboard that is flat on the outside and has a corrugated or ridged core. You can salvage shipping cartons from supermarkets or liquor stores and cut them to the proper size.

On the corrugated cardboard measure off with the ruler and mark with the pencil three 11-inch squares. (It doesn't matter if the cardboard has printing or other marks on it.) Using the metal-edged ruler or steel straightedge as a guide, cut out the three squares with the utility knife. Put the protective board on top of your worktable and make firm, straight downward cuts against it. Repeat the strokes if necessary, holding the ruler or straightedge in place until each cut has been completed.

Now you must stick the three squares of cardboard together with rubber cement with the corrugations running in alternate directions. This will give the base extra strength. First, brush a thin coat of rubber cement on one side of all three squares of cardboard and allow it to dry. Next, turn one of the three cardboard squares over and coat it with cement on the other side also; allow it to dry. This double-coated board is to be the center layer of the three-layer sandwich, and the direction of its corrugations should run in the opposite direction to that of the top and bottom layers. Two rubber-cement–coated surfaces will stick together tightly the instant they touch, so put the three layers together very slowly and accurately. There is no way you can change or adjust the position afterward.

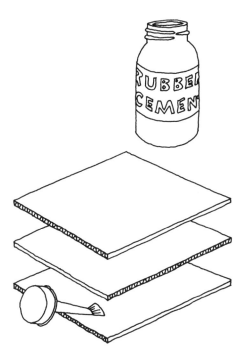

Use the 11-inch square of heavy white paper to make a pattern for the shape of the base. First, with the ruler and pencil draw the diagonals of the square from corner to corner, as shown in the diagram. Then measure and mark a pencil dot $3^{1}/_{4}$ inches from each corner on each of the four sides of the square. Join these dots with ruled lines, as shown, to form a hexagon. Mea-

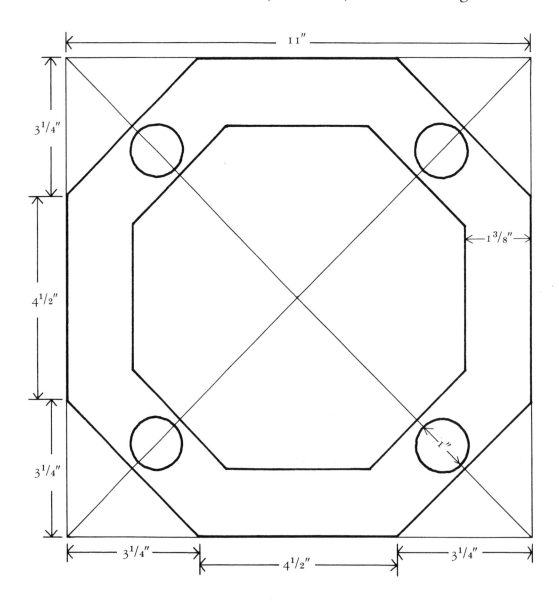

sure in, toward the center $1^3/_8$ inches from each of the eight sides of the hexagon and draw eight lines parallel to the outer lines to mark the lines where the inner area of the base is to be cut out. Where the diagonal lines cross the rim of the base, use the pencil compass to make circles to mark the four places where the four candle-holders will go. Set the point and pencil tip of the compass $1/_2$ inch apart. Measure in $11/_{16}$ inch from the edge of the rim and make a pencil mark on each diagonal line. Draw the four 1-inch circles, centering them on the marks.

Now, starting in the center of each circle, use the sharp-pointed scissors to cut out the four small circles. Then cut out the outer and inner hexagons on the drawn lines. The pattern is hex-agonal and not round for a good reason. Cutting curved lines through three layers of corrugated cardboard would be difficult. Straight knife cuts are much easier to make. Of course, the finished wreath with the greenery in place will appear to be circular in shape.

Put the white-paper pattern on top of the laminated cardboards and tape it in place. With the pencil draw around the outer corners, the inner edge, and the circular holes, and remove the pattern. Hold the utility knife against the metal-edged ruler, or straightedge, and cut out the smaller inner hexagon of the wreath base. Finish the cuts from the back of the base if nec-essary, making repeated, neat, straight-down cuts against the ruler edge. Now cut off the four

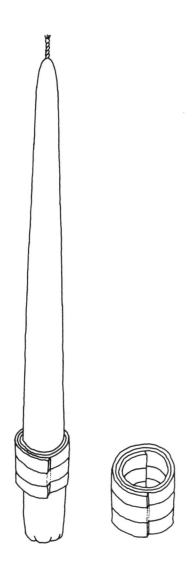

outer corners of the laminated cardboard, pressing the ruler or straightedge very firmly against the board and holding it in place until each cut has been completely made.

Making the Four Candleholders

The candleholders are made from little rolled-up tubes of shirtboard-weight cardboard. Measure, mark off, and cut with the scissors four strips of cardboard 1 by 8 inches. Cut up pieces of masking tape as listed here, and stick the tabs along the edge of your table, where they can easily be pulled off and used. You will need four pieces of tape 5 inches long, four little tabs $1/4$ inch long, and for each candleholder, three pieces of masking tape about $2^1/4$ inches long, cut lengthwise down the center of the tape to make six narrow strips.

Use one of the candles to see what size the tubes for the holders should be. Roll the cardboard strip around the widest part of the candle base. Don't roll it up too tightly, for the candle must slip out easily—and slip in again later as easily, of course. Fasten the rolled-up tube together by wrapping the 5-inch piece of tape around it. Remove the candle, and with a $1/4$-inch tab of tape, fasten the free end of the cardboard inside the tube. Make the other three candleholders in the same way.

Now stand one of the candleholders on end directly on top of one of the marked circles on the cardboard base, and fasten it in place by running one of the narrow strips of tape down the side of the little tube and out onto the surface of the base. Then put another strip directly opposite the first. Press the four remaining pieces of tape down firmly in different supporting positions around the tube. Two should go down over the edge, as shown in the drawing. This will make a very firm attachment for the candleholder. Fasten the three remaining candleholders in the same way.

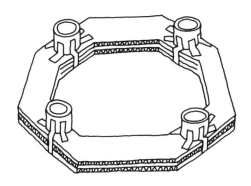

After you have completed your wreath, the cardboard base will be almost entirely covered with evergreens, but to make it as unobtrusive as possible, you should now paint the base with the green poster paint. Apply the paint rather thickly and cover the top surface and edges of the base as well as the outsides and top edges of the candleholders. When the paint is thoroughly dry, you are almost ready to add the evergreens. But, first, to make it easier to attach them, punch holes all the way through the three layers of the base, scattering them over the surface so that they are about two inches apart. The best way to do this is to place the base of the wreath flat on the table with the spot to be punched extending beyond the table. Press down firmly with the awl or the ice pick to make the holes go completely through the laminated base.

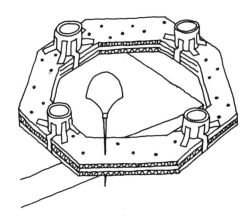

Adding the Evergreens
to the Wreath

You will need a generous amount of evergreen sprigs to cover the base, so go outdoors searching for them and use the pruning shears to collect a carton full of snippets. Branch tips with slender stems are best. Hemlock and spruce are probably the most commonly available evergreens, but unfortunately they have a tendency to shed their needles rather quickly in a warm room. Among the longer-lasting evergreens are white pine, fir, juniper, and arbor vitae. Each variety has a different appearance—short needled, long needled, flat and lacy, round and stiff.

From left to right, white pine and arbor vitae. On opposite page, spruce and hemlock.

Greens of all kinds need to be conditioned before you use them. Put whole branches in a quantity of water in a sink or bathtub overnight. This will wash off any dirt, and if the pieces are frozen, they will gradually thaw. But mainly all the stems will take a big drink of water that will help them to last longer indoors.

Sort out the greens and trim them, cutting off and discarding heavy stems and stumpy ends. Pieces measuring between 3 and 6 inches in length are the easiest to work with. Fasten two or three small sprigs together with about 20 inches of florist's wire, keeping them flat, and leave two ends of wire about 9 or 10 inches long. Even though the wire is very fine, always use wire-cutting pliers or nippers, not scissors, to cut it.

Start adding sprigs to the base by laying the greens flat against the cardboard with their stems near the center of the base and their tips pointing upward and either slightly outward or inward. Stick the ends of the wires through separate holes to the back, or stick one end through a hole and wrap the other end around an edge of the base. Twist the wires together on the back of the wreath. As you work, turn the base in a counterclockwise direction. Continue wiring small bunches of evergreens together and add them to the wreath, so that the stems point downward and the tips of each new bunch cover and conceal the stem ends of the sprigs already attached. All the little branches should head in

Wreath base with the corrugated board partly painted and the first branch fastened in place

the same general direction. This system will make a much more orderly-looking wreath than if the branches went every which way. The varied natural growth of branches will keep the wreath from looking too stiff or formal.

Use the awl or ice pick to poke more holes through the base if you find you need more places to fasten wire. Conceal the wires under the greens as much as possible. Use plenty of evergreens, so that the wreath will not look skimpy, and arrange them so that the outer and inner edges of the wreath are not too smooth and regular in outline. Avoid pruning the tips of the sprigs as much as you can. The stems of the final bunch of greens should be tucked under the tips of the first bunch you attached so that nowhere are there any stem ends showing.

At last, if you want to add a few small pine cones, you must furnish each cone with its own wire fastener. Pass the center section of the wire around the base of the cone, under the first row of petals, twisting the wire tightly together where the two pieces meet. Then use the free ends to fasten the cone to the wreath.

When all the materials have been attached and arranged to your satisfaction, turn the wreath over carefully and snip off all the ends of wire; press the twists flat against the back with the pliers. Coat the whole back of the wreath with rubber cement. To make the backing of felt or heavy cotton, use the same paper pattern you made for the base. Fold it in half, pin it to

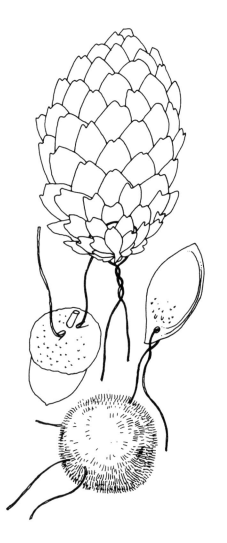

the folded 11-inch square of felt (with the folded edges matching), and cut out the cloth, ignoring the candle holes. Coat one side of the cloth lightly with rubber cement, and when the cement is dry, press the cloth backing in place on the base. It will cover all the wires and give a neat finish to the bottom of your wreath.

After you have added the four bright-red candles to your finished wreath, we think you will agree that they look very attractive, rising out of the circlet of greens. Soft candlelight adds a warm glow to any Christmas table.

Other Wreaths You Can Make

You can use the same corrugated cardboard base to make at least two variations of this wreath—without the Advent candles. One is a wreath made entirely of pine cones; the other a wreath made principally of dried seedpods, sycamore balls, nuts, and cones. Every variety of seedpod or nut you use must have a hole pierced through it, made by an awl or heavy, sharp needle or drilled with a $1/16$-inch drill bit, in order to make a place where you can put a wire to attach it to the piece. Although these wreaths are made on the same kind of corrugated cardboard base as the Advent wreath, you need not paint the cardboard green. The finished wreath should be protected with a light coating of spray lacquer (such as Krylon or Testor's). If you like, you can put a fat red or green candle in the center of either wreath.

You can also make a delicate miniature wreath about $3\frac{1}{2}$ inches in diameter on this same kind of base. Use two laminated thicknesses of shirtboard or other lightweight cardboard and paint the cardboard green. Tiny sprigs of flat, lacy arbor vitae are good for small wreaths, and you might want to add a tiny red-velvet bow to each. Make a number of them to encircle the base of each tumbler or goblet on the dinner table. Each guest will later want to take his or her little wreath home.

If you want to make a larger wreath to hang on a door or wall, the flat cardboard base used for table wreaths will be too flimsy and flat. It would be better to buy a floral-foam wreath base or a sturdy wire one on which a heavier and deeper wreath can be shaped. Florist- and garden-supply shops have several sizes of wreath forms, wide ribbons for bows, floral tape, florist's picks, wire, and other essentials for wreath making.

At the beginning of Advent it was the custom for young Polish girls to cut a branch from a cherry tree, bring it indoors, and put it in a vase of water. If the branch bloomed on Christmas Eve, the maiden who had cut the branch was sure to find a husband within a year.

2
THE AUSTRIAN
ZWETSCHKEN
KRAMPUS

An edible Christmas devil

The first colonists to sail into the harbors of Virginia and Massachusetts in the seventeenth century were the English coming to seek their fortunes in a strange land. Before long, settlers from other countries arrived on the small wooden sailing ships that had braved the long voyage across the vast Atlantic Ocean. The adventurers all came hoping for a chance at a new life, but all of them brought their native traditions, customs, and religious beliefs. The people of each land also had their own ways of celebrating Christmas; some of those ways now, three and a half centuries later, have been almost forgotten in the United States.

In many parts of the Old World where Christmas was celebrated, St. Nicholas, who is known by many names, was not the only legendary visitor who arrived during the Christmas season. Santa Claus, as we Americans call the good saint who brings us gifts, was often pre-

16

ceded or accompanied by prankish characters quite unlike him—sprites or elves who played tricks on children, sometimes frightening and threatening to punish them. In a few lands, this December visitor represented the devil, and *he,* of course, scared everybody!

For children today Christmas in America is customarily a time of great joy and happiness. The "bad" or threatening Christmas spirits have simply vanished from our celebration. But many generations of European children did and still do believe in them. In Germany there is a strange old gnome called *Belsnickle* or *Pelsnickle,* meaning "Nicholas dressed in fur." In Denmark he is a mischief-maker named *Nisse,* who is accompanied by his cat. Danish children put out a saucer of milk on Christmas Eve, knowing that the milk will be gone by the following morn-

In the center of this Danish Christmas-tree ornament is a tiny Julenisse, *a Christmas elf, made of wire wrapped with red yarn.* From the United Nations Headquarters Gift Center, New York City.

ing. In Sweden *Juletomten* is a protective little gnome who brings good luck. In Finland the sprite is represented by a playful goat named *Joukupukki,* whom the children like to imitate. At Christmastime they don long-nosed masks with curving horns and chin whiskers, fit paper hooves on their shoes, and prance around the house. The Norwegians call their frisky goat a *Julebukk,* and in that country as well as in Finland, craftsmen make little long-horned goats of straw at Christmas. The goat was originally the symbolic pet of the Norse god, Thor, who was worshiped centuries ago by Norsemen.

In Holland St. Nicholas comes before

A Norwegian Julebukk,
the Christmas goat,
made of wheat straw tied with red yarn

Christmas, dressed in bishop's robes, wearing a tall pointed miter on his head and carrying a crozier. *Sinterklaas,* the Dutch name for Saint Nicholas, gave us our words Santa Claus. But it was the bishop's servant, Black Peter, in his ugly black mask, carrying not only a sackful of toys but a threatening bundle of birch rods, who knew which children had been good all year and which bad.

For centuries in a number of European countries, and especially in Austria, children have been told about *Krampus,* a black devil similar to Black Peter, who comes according to legend to check up on children on St. Nicholas's Day, December sixth. *Krampus* clumps heavily through the streets at night, dressed all in black fur, wearing a frightful black wig with two big black horns. His face is blackened; his fierce eyes flash; and he has a pointed red tongue that hangs down to his waist. *Krampus* carries a *Rute,* or bundle of switches, in each hand and has a long heavy chain around his neck. When children imagine they hear him clanking along in the night, they feel very scared because they have been told, "If you don't behave, *Krampus* will come and stuff you into the *Bütte* on his back. He will carry you away to his underworld forever!"

In Austria this figure is also fashioned into a traditional sweet, made of dark-colored dried fruit. The *Zwetschken Krampus,* or "prune devil," is sometimes ten or twelve inches tall and can be bought in fancy food shops. You can construct a large one, or if you prefer, you can make a smaller and simpler *Krampus* of the sort Austrian children often made for themselves. No matter what size *Krampus* an Austrian child has at Christmastime, in the end the devil is eaten up, and thus the evil spirit disappears, and good fortune will follow. The photographs show two versions of the *Zwetschken Krampus,* made from memory by two women who grew up in Vienna; they remember *Krampus* and his noisy chain very well, and both of them say they are still afraid of him!

The little Krampus (*left*) *made by Gertrude Rys.*
The big Krampus (*right*) *made by Yvonne Forbath.*

It is very easy to construct either of these half-funny, half-scary-looking little figures out of dried fruit, wire, toothpicks, broomstraws, colored paper, and a chain. In spite of his unsavory reputation, when you eat your Christmas *Krampus,* you will discover he is quite delicious!

The Little Krampus

This figure can be put together so easily and quickly that you may want to make several and use them as tie-on ornaments for packages. Or you can hang them from cord loops to use as Christmas-tree decorations. You can also make an unusual gift by putting three or four little devils in a box on a bed of wax paper and enclosing a tiny handmade book with a nicely lettered story about *Krampus.* Be sure to explain that good luck will come to the person who eats the little devils!

The *Krampus* in the left-hand photograph is only $4^1/4$ inches tall, but the height of the one you make will depend on the size of the fruit you use. The best prunes or figs to use are the small, very hard dried ones you can buy in city delicatessens and gourmet shops where imported sweets are sold. Prunes and figs packaged in foil-lined cartons and available in supermarkets are also fine. Do not, however, use fruit that comes packed in plastic bags; it is usually too moist and soft.

Materials and Tools
for the Little Krampus

SMALL DRIED PRUNES OR FIGS. You will need ten hard dark pieces of fruit.

TOOTHPICKS, about eight round white wooden ones

POCKETKNIFE or paring knife

SCISSORS

RED PAPER, small strip, for the tongue

FELT PEN, black, with a fine point

BLACK PAPER (optional), small stiff piece, for the horns

BROOM STRAWS, a few, to make the bundle of switches

THREAD, ordinary sewing weight

TRANSPARENT TAPE

CHAIN, lightweight piece, 4 or 5 inches long

Look at the photographs and drawings, and begin by putting the feet, legs, body, and arms together by sticking a toothpick through each two adjoining pieces of fruit. Do not try to remove the prune pits. Just work the toothpick lengthwise through the prunes, bypassing the pits. The toothpicks should not show, so cut off with the knife or scissors any ends that stick out.

After you have made the body, choose one fruit to be used for the head. To make the features of the face, cut a pointed tongue out of red paper—it can be one or two inches long. Use

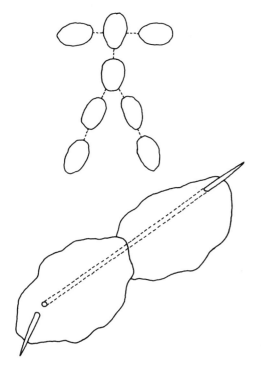

the snipped-off end of a toothpick to attach it to the face.

To make the eyes, cut out with the knife two sections about $^3/_8$ inch long from the center of two of the toothpicks. Trim one end of each section so that is smooth but slightly rounded, and with the felt pen make a black dot in the center of the rounded ends to represent the two eyes. Press these pieces into the fruit leaving a fraction of an inch of the marked ends protruding, so that your *Krampus* has two rather buggy eyes.

You can make the horns in one of two ways. Either you can cut a prune or fig into horn-shaped pieces and attach them to the sides of the head with two short pieces of toothpick, as in the photograph; or you can cut out two horns from stiff black paper and stick them into slits cut in the head. Use a toothpick to attach another small fruit or half fruit on top of the head to represent bushy black hair.

Cut up the broom straws into slightly different lengths of about 2 or $2^1/_2$ inches and with the thread bind them together very tightly at one end. Make a hole in one hand of the *Krampus* with the point of the scissors and stick the little bundle of switches into the hole. Press the fruit together around the straws. If the bundle will not stay in place, use a small piece of transparent tape to fasten it, preferably at the back.

The chain can be a small piece from old costume jewelry, a piece of chain from a hardware

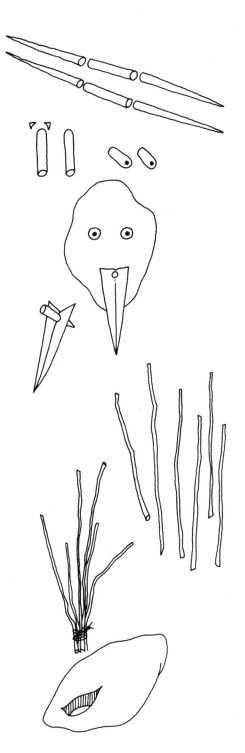

store, or a key chain. Loop it around the hands or neck of the *Krampus* in any way you wish.

To make the figure stand up, stick one end of a toothpick into his lower back at an angle, so that the other end of the toothpick can rest on the table behind him and help to keep his balance.

The Big Krampus

There are two important differences between the small and the large figures. The big *Krampus* would wobble and probably not stand up if he were put together with toothpicks. So you need to build the figure on a strong wire support or skeleton, called an armature. Secondly, the large figure could not be made to stand up straight just by leaning him on a toothpick, so the lower ends of the wire armature in the legs must be fastened to a flat base. This will give your tall prune devil a very firm stance.

Materials and Tools for the Big Krampus

DRIED PRUNES, twenty-three, for the arms, legs, neck, and hat

DRIED FIGS, five large flat brown ones, for the body and head

DRIED APRICOTS, two, for the face and the back
of the head

A CANDIED OR MARASCHINO CHERRY or red
gumdrop for the eyes and mouth

CLOVES, two whole ones, for the eyes

DRIED DATES, two, for the feet

STEEL WIRE, 14 gauge. You will need two
pieces 14 inches long and one piece $3^{1}/_{2}$
inches long, clipped from the roll in which
it is sold.

RULER

WIRE-CUTTING PLIERS or nippers

FELT PEN, black, with a fine point

VISE

BULL-NOSE PLIERS

POCKETKNIFE or paring knife

TOOTHPICKS, five or six round white wooden
ones

RED PAPER, strip about $^{1}/_{2}$ inch wide by 5
inches long, for the tongue

SCISSORS, sharp-pointed

BLACK PAPER, small stiff square about $1^{1}/_{2}$
inches wide, for the horns

BROOM STRAWS, a few, about 3 inches long, to
make the bundle of switches; or, alternately,
two cinnamon sticks, to represent cudgels in
the hands

THREAD, ordinary sewing weight

TRANSPARENT TAPE

CHAIN, 12 or 14 inches long. You can buy inexpensive lightweight brass chain by the foot
in hardware stores.

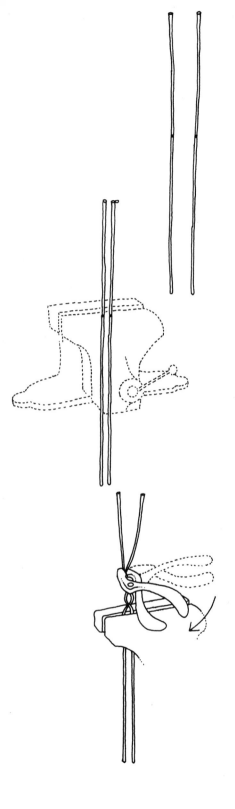

Making an Armature
for the Figure

Earlier we mentioned that the armature is a support or skeleton made of wire or other stiff material over which the *Krampus,* or for that matter, any piece of sculpture made out of a soft material can be shaped. In this case, instead of forming clay over the armature, you simply string the fruit on the shaped wire in much the same way as you string beads.

The armature is made of two pieces of stiff wire twisted together tightly near the center. Clip from the roll of wire two pieces 14 inches long, using the wire-cutting pliers or nippers. Measure $7^1/2$ inches in from one end of each piece of wire and make a mark there with the felt pen. Clamp the two wires tightly in the vise, placing them side by side. Clamp them on the marks with the $7^1/2$-inch ends pointing downward. The vise will hold the wires firmly while you twist them with the pliers.

Holding the heavy pliers in your right hand, pinch the two wires together just above the jaws of the vise. Move the pliers to the left in order to twist the two wires together in a quarter turn. Release the wires, move them up a fraction of an inch, clamp the wires again, and give them another quarter turn. Continue moving the wires upward, making a continuous, tightly twisted section about $1^1/2$ inches long. This will serve as the framework for the torso,

26

or central part, of the figure. The $7^1/_2$-inch ends of wire will make the legs. The ends above the twist will later be bent apart to be used for the arms. When you have finished twisting the wires, while they are still clamped in the vise, straighten out the two ends above the twist so that they are close together pointing straight up. Remove the armature from the vise; the skeleton for your figure is now done.

Covering the Armature

Separate the lower ends of the leg wires for about $1^1/_2$ inches and start pushing the prunes lengthwise onto the two wires. If you work in the direction of the length of the fruit, bypassing the pits, the wires will go easily through the fruit. Put the prunes on both leg wires, using five to each leg. Push them up firmly against the twisted wire for the torso. Do not put the feet on yet.

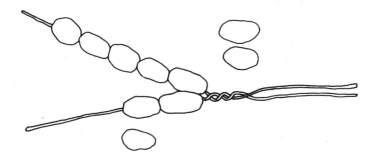

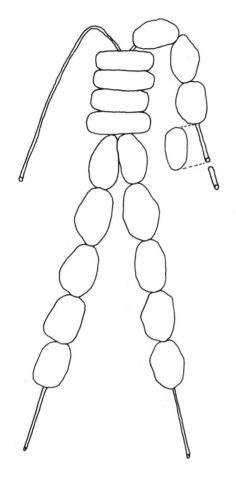

Holding the wires together at the top as if they were one, push four figs crosswise onto the wires, as in the photograph. Press the figs down firmly so that they join the prunes that form the legs. Now you can separate the wires at the top of the figs and bend them out with the pliers to make the arms. String four prunes on each wire, and if you see that the wire will be so long that it will go entirely through the last prune (the one representing the hand), clip off the extra wire so that it does not show. Before putting the last prune on each arm, bend the wires forward a little, about $1/2$ inch from each end, so that the hands will seem to hold the switches or cudgels naturally.

Now cut a piece of wire $3^1/2$ inches long to serve as a framework for the neck which will join the head to the body. On this wire, following the photograph, put on one prune for the neck, leaving about $3/4$ inch of wire below the fruit.

Making the Head

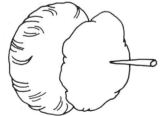

The head is made of one round flat fig with an apricot fastened flat in the center for the face, and another fastened at the back of the fig to round out the head a little. Use a short piece of toothpick to attach the apricot in the center of the fig. For the eyes, cut out two small, round pieces of red candied or Maraschino cherry or

gumdrop about $1/4$ inch across and stick them on with the two whole cloves. Fold the strip of red paper down the center and cut out a pointed tongue about $1/4$ inch wide (when folded) and 5 inches long; cut off the "mouth" end square. Unfold and half flatten out the piece and attach it to the face by putting the top of the strip of red paper under a small chunk of cherry or gumdrop and sticking them both on with the clipped-off tip of a toothpick. Cut two pointed horns out of the black paper, and insert the square ends in two knife-slits in the head.

Now stick the neck wire straight up through the head, add another prune on top, and trim off the wire if it sticks up too far—or press the wire down. Attach the head section to the body with the lower end of the same wire. Add the apricot to the back of the head by putting a small prune over the upper half of it and sticking them both on with a section of toothpick. Add one more prune to each side of the head with toothpicks to complete the appearance of bushy black hair.

29

Attaching the
Switches or Cudgels

If you want to have your *Krampus* hold a bundle
of switches in each hand, cut the broom straws
2$^1/_2$ or 3 inches long, and make two small bunches, binding each of them together tightly at
one end with thread. With the point of the scissors make holes or slits about $^1/_4$ inch deep in
each of the hands and insert the bundles, pressing the fruit around them. Secure the bundles at
the back with transparent tape, if necessary. If
you prefer to use two cinnamon sticks as
cudgels, they can be stuck entirely through the
hands, as shown in the photograph.

Making the Base

You can make a wooden base for your *Krampus*
like the one in the photograph, or if you prefer,
you can make a simpler one out of several layers
of cardboard. The wooden base looks more
handsome but requires more tools. A thick
cardboard base will also serve to hold the figure
upright, even though it will look less permanent and finished than a wooden one.

Materials and Tools
for a Wooden Base

PINE BOARD, or any other softwood. You will
need a piece $^3/_4$ inch thick by 3 inches wide
by 3$^1/_2$ inches long

RULER

PENCIL

VISE

HAND SAW, crosscut or hacksaw

SANDPAPER, fine, No. 120 or 3/0

FELT PEN, black, with a fine point

HAND DRILL with a $5/64$-inch bit; or, alternately, a hammer and a 4-penny finishing nail

WIRE-CUTTING PLIERS OR NIPPERS

EPOXY GLUE

On the pine board, measure off with the ruler and mark with the pencil a rectangle with the 3-inch dimension going across the grain of the wood and the $3\frac{1}{2}$-inch dimension going with the grain, or lengthwise. Put the board in the vise to hold it firmly, with the marks facing you, and saw carefully on the lines, turning the wood after each cut so as to saw downward. Sandpaper the whole block until it is quite smooth—especially the sawed edges.

Now hold your *Krampus* above the wooden block, so that the wires of the legs touch it. Position the figure so that it appears to be centered but allow enough space in front for the feet, which will be added later. With the felt pen make two dots on the wood base where the holes to accommodate the wires for the legs must be made. If you are going to drill these holes, clamp the wood in the vise with the dots facing you; then drill by pushing the tool away from you. Stop drilling just short of the bottom

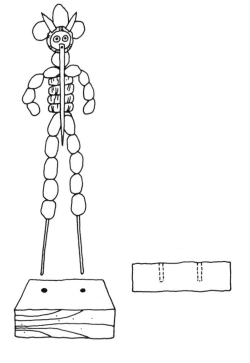

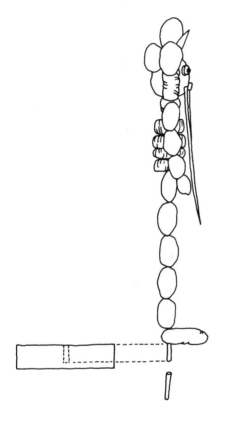

of the block—the wires will stay in place more firmly if the holes do not go all the way through. If you do not have a drill and bit, you can make the holes by hammering a 4-penny finishing nail into the wood on the marked dots. First tap the point of the nail firmly with a hammer to blunt the tip. A blunt nail— believe it or not—will be much less apt to split the wood. In order to pull the nail out afterward, clamp the nail itself in the vise, and twist off the piece of wood, pulling straight out as you twist. This will leave a neat straight hole.

Put the dates for the feet on the wires, pointing forward, of course, and push them up against the prune legs. Try fitting the wires in the holes now to make sure the length is right, and with the wire-cutting pliers or nippers clip off any extra wire. Using the little tab on the top of one of the tubes, mix together a very small amount of epoxy glue in a small dish or on a piece of wax paper, in accordance with the directions on the tube. The two kinds of goo must be mixed together in equal amounts before they become adhesive. Again, using the little tab, smear some of the glue on each wire, stick the wire into the holes in the base, press down well, and stand the figure aside to allow the glue to dry overnight.

Immediately wipe any remaining glue from the necks of the tubes, out of the dish, and from your hands, using a dry rag. When hard, the glue cannot be removed, but while soft it can be wiped away with a cloth. The solvent for still-soft epoxy glue is denatured (wood) alcohol or lacquer thinner.

When the glue has dried, your *Krampus* is finished except for the chain, which you can place around his neck or in any way you wish.

Materials and Tools for a Cardboard Base

CARDBOARD, very stiff and heavy (but not corrugated). You will need at least two 4-inch squares, or four or more pieces of lighter cardboard.

RULER

PENCIL

STIFF CARD, such as an index card

RAZOR BLADE, single-edged

FELT PEN, black, with a fine point

HAMMER

FINISHING NAIL, one 4-penny

POSTER PAINT

PAINTBRUSH, size No. 3 or No. 4

EPOXY GLUE

PLIERS

TRANSPARENT TAPE

CLOTHESPINS, four, spring-clip type

SANDPAPER, fine, No. 120 or 3/0

This lighter and thinner base is a little simpler to make and will serve the purpose. On the heaviest piece of plain cardboard you can find, carefully measure off with the ruler and mark with the pencil two or more squares 4 by 4 inches. Use a corner of the stiff card to guide you in making the corners true. These cardboard squares are to be laminated, or glued together, to make a sturdy base that is $3/16$ inch thick. Cut out the cardboard squares on the lines, using a ruler and a single-edged razor blade—put a piece of wooden board underneath while cutting, to protect your worktable. Stack up the cutout pieces and see if their combined thickness measures $3/16$ inch. If not, cut more squares of cardboard until the base is the proper thickness.

Hold the figure of the *Krampus* upright (without feet) in the center of one of the squares of cardboard, leaving enough space in front for the feet to be added later. Mark with the felt pen the spots where the wires touch the cardboard. Make holes that go through *one half* of the stacked-up cardboards you are going to use; that is, through one layer if you are using two, through two layers if you are using four, and so on. Using the 4-penny nail and hammer, pound the holes through the cardboard against a wooden board.

Give the surface of the top piece of punched cardboard one or two coats of poster paint in whatever color you like, waiting for the first coat to dry before applying the second. When the paint is dry, mix up about a teaspoonful of epoxy glue, as directed on the tube. Now you need to glue together the punched layers of cardboard, or half the pieces you plan to use to make up the ³/₁₆-inch thickness. Spread glue thinly on the facing surfaces of each piece of punched cardboard and press these layers together with the painted piece on top. Put the dates for the feet on the wires in the right position and stick the ends of the wire through the holes you punched in the glued layers of cardboard. Push the cardboard up, until the date feet are tight against the prunes. With pliers, grasp the ends of the wires, one at a time, where they stick through the cardboard and bend each wire into a sharp right angle. The end of one wire should go toward one corner of the base, and the end of the other wire should go toward the opposite corner. This will give the standing figure better balance. Secure the bent wires flat against the cardboard with transparent tape.

Lay the *Krampus* on his back on the table with the base sticking out over the table edge. Spread glue thinly on one surface of each of the remaining squares of cardboard and stick all the pieces together, thus securing the wires in the center of the stack. Wipe off any extra glue with the rag. Clamp the four edges of the square base together with the spring-clip clothespins and allow the cardboard to remain overnight at the edge of the table with the clothespins in place. The next day, remove the clamps. Then sandpaper the edges of the base and touch them up with paint.

Now your prune devil is finished, you may

35

want to adjust his position a little by bending the wire skeleton. Handle the fruit carefully as you do so. Put the chain over his hand or around his neck. Your completed *Zwetschken Krampus* looks dark and scary, and a little clownish, too, just like those that have been eaten by generations of European children. Your *Krampus* will be much admired during the Christmas season—as long as he lasts!

Swiss children believe their Christmas gifts are brought to them by Christkindli, *or the Christ child, who comes as an angel, dressed all in white, wearing a golden crown and carrying a magic wand.*

It is the kindly St. Nicholas who brings gifts to Belgian children, who believe he comes riding on a horse. So on the eve of December sixth young people always leave hay, carrots, and water for the horse outside the house.

Many years ago in France children put their heavy wooden shoes, called sabots, *in front of the fireplace on Christmas Eve, waiting for them to be filled with gifts from* le Père Nöel *or* le Petit Jésus—*Father Christmas or little Jesus.*

3
AN ENGLISH KISSING BALL

Christmas under the mistletoe

The doorways and entrance halls of hundreds upon hundreds of homes are decorated at holiday time with a bunch of mistletoe tied with red ribbon. One of the most cheerfully practiced customs at Christmas and New Year's is "kissing under the mistletoe." Many people know that the delicate green sprigs with their translucent white berries are said to have magical powers and that anyone has the right to plant an affectionate kiss upon the cheek of the person who stands, even for a moment, under it. Nowadays we associate mistletoe almost exclusively with Christmastime, but the legends about it began long before the birth of Christ. And there is still a lingering mystery about how it came to be connected with kissing.

This rather delicate climbing shrub has a very long history. Many, many centuries ago in the British Isles there was a group of people known as the Druids, who were much revered and had many special privileges. Candidates for

this sacred order were required to spend twenty years studying and preparing themselves to be admitted to it. The members were a mixture of priest, judge, doctor, and magician. The Druids were so much respected that in their presence no one else dared to be the first to speak.

The mistletoe plant was held sacred by the Druids, and the oak forests in which it grew were the retreats or temples of the chosen men. The shrub is actually a parasite, meaning that it lives and gets its nourishment by attaching its long vinelike tendrils to a stronger growing plant or tree. This makes it comparatively rare, and whenever the sacred plant was found, it was cut with a golden knife by the arch Druid, or high priest, and was never allowed to fall on the ground. Mysterious ceremonies accompanied the cutting of the plant, and the sprigs were distributed among the people, who kept them as a magic talisman. Druids wore mistletoe woven into garlands of leaves to ward off evil spirits, and the juice of the berries was used to make medicines that served as remedies for poisons. Finally, during the hundred years or so before Christ, the Roman invaders conquered the last of the Druids, cut down the sacred forests, and put an end to the secret practices. The Druid cult eventually disappeared, but their ancient reverence for mistletoe survived. The green sprig gradually came to be linked—somewhat inexplicably—with the Christmas season, and today mistletoe is used as a decoration in homes, but never in Christian churches.

The Scandinavian countries have their own legend about the plant that may be more directly related to our custom of kissing under the mistletoe. A Norse legend says that the waxen white berries were formed by the tears shed by Freya, the goddess of love and beauty, after her son Balder was wounded by a dart made of mistletoe. When he finally recovered, it was decreed that the plant could never again be used for evil purposes, and afterward it was believed that the goddess would bestow a secret kiss upon anyone who passed under the mistletoe.

In England in the nineteenth century, when kissing under the mistletoe was an established custom, each boy who kissed a girl plucked off a white berry and gave it to the young lady. When all the berries were gone, the plant's magic was gone, too, and no more kissing could take place. The British called their decoration a "kissing bough" or "kissing bunch," and it was at first an elaborate, large hanging ornament with lighted candles, apples, and greens surrounding the mistletoe. Undoubtedly it was settlers from England who brought a simplified kissing ball to the New World.

In America it is the custom to hang the sprigs of mistletoe in a bunch alone or to tie them inside an open, globe-shaped frame. A kissing ball is a very simple decoration to make. You can construct an airy little "cage" from two crisscrossed and wrapped embroidery hoops to make a holder for the evergreens and mistletoe. The kissing custom adds gaiety and fun to the

The finished kissing ball, made by the author

more formal joys of the holiday season, and it is a pretty interpretation of a very old tradition.

Materials and Tools for the Kissing Ball

MISTLETOE, one bunch—or more—from a florist or supermarket

RUG YARN, one hank (about 4 ounces), in bright red or green. You can buy either heavy cotton or Orlon yarn in packages that are sometimes labeled craft yarn. One hank will make several kissing balls. (We think red looks best.)

EMBROIDERY HOOPS. You will need a pair of metal or wooden hoops, 6 or 7 inches in diameter.

SCISSORS

TRANSPARENT TAPE

TWEEZERS, preferably with pointed ends

RULER

FLORIST'S WIRE, No. 30

WIRE-CUTTING PLIERS or nippers

SPRIGS OF EVERGREEN (optional), one or two

RIBBON. You can use red or green velvet, satin, or grosgrain ribbon, either $3/4$ or 1 inch wide. You will need about $2^{1}/_{3}$ yards. The sort of shiny ribbon used to wrap gifts is too flimsy and curls up too much to hang well.

BELLS (optional), a few of the tiny ones used to decorate packages

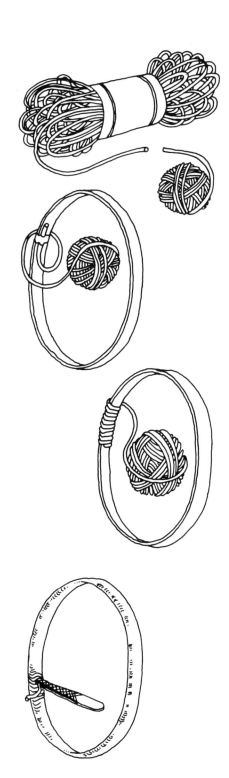

Winding the Embroidery Hoops with Yarn

Leaving the paper wrapping on the hank, start with the free end to wind the yarn into a fairly tight ball a little smaller than a tennis ball. Cut off the end of the yarn and set aside the hank. Separate the two embroidery hoops and with the transparent tape fasten the free end of the ball of yarn to the inner side of the smaller of the two hoops. Wind the yarn back over the tape to hide it, then continue to wind the yarn firmly and neatly around the rest of the hoop, covering it completely. As you work, you will have to pass the ball of yarn through the hoop. This is a bit awkward at first, but you will soon get the rhythm of it. Work close to the ball of yarn; do not allow a long piece of yarn to string out from the ball.

When you have reached the wrapped starting point, cut off the yarn leaving an end about 2 inches long. Twist the end tightly and grasp it between the points of the tweezers. Using the tweezers, tuck the end under the wrapping to conceal it.

Wind the yarn around the outer hoop in the same way, starting at the edge of the spring or screw. Cover the hoop completely except for the spring or screw. Conceal the end of the yarn again with the tweezers. The small area now left uncovered will be the top of the kissing ball, and will be hidden as described below.

42

Tying the
Globe Together

To tie the two hoops together, slip the inner hoop inside the outer one, so that they are in a crosswise position. Adjust them to form a straight, right-angled crossing. If you are using metal hoops, the spring that holds the outer hoop together will "give" enough to allow you to put the smaller hoop in position; then it will tighten and hold firmly. Wooden hoops have a small metal hand screw on the outer one; loosen the screw and place the two hoops at a right angle, then turn it clockwise to tighten and hold both hoops in place.

Cut two lengths of yarn about 30 inches long. Starting with the center of one piece, make an X-shaped wrapping around the joint at the top of the hoop. To finish, tie the ends of the yarn together in a knot on the inside of the hoops and leave ends about 2 inches long. With tweezers secure the ends in the wrappings as before. Repeat the "X" tie at the other, lower joint of the hoops.

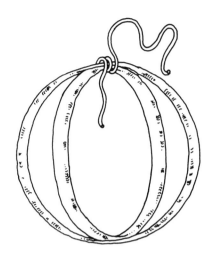

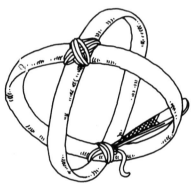

Adding the Mistletoe,
Greens, and Ribbon Decoration

Using florist's wire to fasten the stems together, arrange the bunch of mistletoe. If the sprigs look a little skimpy, add a few bits of evergreen

or laurel leaves to fill out the shape of the ball nicely. (See the instructions in Chapter 1 for conditioning greens before use.) Keep trying the arrangement inside the ball, with stems *up*. The bottom of the hanging mistletoe and other greens should come just above the lower joint of the framework.

When the greens have been arranged and fastened together, use another piece of wire about 20 inches long to attach the bunch to the top joint of the hoops. Twist the wires together to make a firm attachment and clip off any extra wire. To make a hanger, cut still another piece of wire about 3 feet long and fold it into thirds to make a three-strand hanger 12 inches long. Twist the ends of the triple strand together and wind the center of the strand once around the top joint of the globe. You can then twist about 2 inches of the free ends together to make a loop, or you can leave the ends free to wrap around a hook or chandelier.

Cut a piece of the ribbon about 34 inches long and tie a single, generous bow around the joint at the top of the ball, leaving the hanger wire free. The long ends of the bow will hang gracefully inside the ball. With the remaining 50-inch piece of ribbon tie a double bow (one bow on top of another) around the joint at the bottom of the globe. Make the bow on the outside of the ball. Allow the loops of the bow and the ends of the ribbon to hang free. You can sew tiny bells near the ends of the ribbon streamers if you want to add a modern touch.

44

Presto! Your little hanging ornament is finished just that easily. Sprigs of mistletoe may not ward off evil as the Druids believed, but for anyone who stands under the plant at Christmastime, mistletoe is certainly magical!

The first weekday after Christmas is called Boxing Day in Britain, particularly in rural areas. Little boxes packed with food and sweets or small gifts or coins are given to visitors who call on that day: tenants, gardeners, maids, cooks, tradesmen, and the neighborhood children.

A prank called Hodening *used to be played by children in Wales during the Christmas season. A carved wooden horse's head with big eyes and snaggly teeth was attached to a stick with which the head was carried. Fastened to the head of the "horse" was a sheet, which covered two boys who formed the body of the animal. Groups of such revelers would walk the streets at night trying to frighten people. Often the children were invited in for cakes and cider. Hodening originated in medieval Christmas miracle plays in which there was usually a prankish character who rode a hobbyhorse.*

4
PERUVIAN SANTITOS

Painted Christmas saints from Cuzco

In the Andes Mountains of Peru there is a very old South American city named Cuzco. It was once the principal city of the ancient empire of the Incas. These Indians worshiped the sun, and so they called their capital "City of the Sun." Cuzco is thought to have been founded in the eleventh century by Manco Capac, the Inca leader. His successors were wise and kindly rulers of a kingdom that finally extended beyond the present boundaries of Peru. But in 1533 the Spaniards led by Pizarro conquered all of Peru and introduced the religion, customs, architecture, and language of Spain. Most of the dark-skinned Indians now living in and near Cuzco are descendants of the peace-loving and intelligent natives of long ago. Many live in isolated mountain villages, where they speak only the native Quechua language and wear traditional dress.

As you look down on modern Cuzco, from an airplane or from the surrounding mountainside, the hundreds of red-tiled roofs on the small stucco houses seem to carpet the valley. The city has no very tall buildings, and in its center are some low stone structures—one large cathedral, several government buildings, one or two hotels, and some smaller churches. A few modern edifices in the city stand on foundations of massive, ancient sculptured stones—relics of the Incas, who were master builders. The streets are roughly paved with cobblestones and are very narrow, steep, and winding. The houses are built right next to each other and against the street. The homes and little shops are often in rather bad repair, but many of them have pleasant inner courtyards or patios with a tree or two and some plants and flowers, like the Spanish homes from which they were copied.

On one of the winding streets of the city lives a family of artisans, the Mendivils, who engage in the craft known as "image making." They model little figures of saints. In Cuzco such craftsmen are called *imagineros* and are looked upon as important members of the community.

Three or four generations of the family have carried on the craft. The Mendivils are Peruvian Indians who speak both the Quechua language of their Incan ancestors and the Spanish language of those Incan ancestors' conquerors. Hilario and Georgina Mendivil together with their eleven-year-old son, Hilario, a grandfather, and several aunts, uncles, and cousins all work as

47

Three santitos *from Cuzco, Peru.*
From left to right, the figures
are 5, 5^1/$_2$, and 4^1/$_2$ inches high.

imagineros. The painted plaster *santitos,* or "little
saints," shown in the photographs were made
by hand in the family's cluttered home studio.

The small images the Mendivils make for
Christmas are of the Virgin Mary, the Christian
saints, the Nativity story, and angels. The style
of the little figures is primitive, and the colors
used to paint them are bright hues of red, yellow, blue, and green with touches of shiny
gold. The *santitos* are only four or five inches tall,

and they are turned out by the gross from a variety of plaster molds. Originally all the figures were modeled in clay, and from that the plaster molds were made. They are sold principally in the Indian market and in a few small stores in Cuzco, but they are seldom if ever seen in the more sophisticated shops of Lima, the capital of Peru. In Cuzco the little images can be bought for a few copper coins, and they are the only Christmas decorations that many mountain Indians can afford to buy.

The brightly painted plaster saints have the appeal of all simple folk art. A distinctive characteristic of the Mendivil figures is the elongated neck of the women, which gives them a surprising elegance. The small saints and angels are meant to be seen only from the front; they are usually left unfinished on the back, and after each is fixed to a small, flat base so that it will stand, they are painted, then lacquered. Sometimes the traditional blue robe of the Virginlike angel (the kneeling figure in the photograph) is painted on the back. The *santitos* are usually placed on a small shelf with candles and perhaps a few flowers arranged around them to form a small Christmas shrine. The flat figures of the Christmas *santitos,* however, are not at all like the crèche figures of other countries and do not represent the Nativity scene. They are simply individual saints, and their primitive style is unique and distinctive to Cuzco.

Since the *santitos* are plain on the back and

very simply modeled, it is not at all difficult to reproduce them, using either a "self-hardening" artist's clay or a home-mixed modeling material, both of which are easier to use than plaster. Poster colors and metallic gold liquid paints can be used to decorate them. Even young children can make their own interpretations of these engaging little figures of mixed lineage—part Peruvian and part Spanish.

Materials and Tools for the Santitos

CLAY. You can use one of several brands of permanent, self-hardening modeling clay, sold in art-supply stores, or a homemade cornstarch "clay." (The recipe for the cornstarch mixture is given on pages 52–53.)

WAX PAPER

MODELING TOOLS. You can use either the professional, double-ended modeling tools sold in art-supply stores or any of the following: a manicurist's orangewood stick, a popsicle stick or wooden tongue depressor, or a metal nail file

PARING KNIFE

WOODEN DOWEL, about 8 inches long by $3/4$ or 1 inch in diameter, to roll out the clay

CARDBOARD, shirtboard weight, a piece about 8 by 13 inches

RULER

PENCIL

SCISSORS

WHITE GLUE, Elmer's, Sobo, Ad-A-Grip, or a
similar type

AWL

WIRE-CUTTING PLIERS or nippers

STEEL WIRE, 18 gauge. You will need one piece
13 inches long for each standing figure.

BULL-NOSE PLIERS

NEEDLE-NOSE PLIERS

MASKING TAPE, $1/2$ or $3/4$ inch wide

CLOTHESPINS, six or eight, spring-clip type

FINE SANDPAPER, No. 120 or No. 3/0

POSTER PAINTS. You will need six colors: red,
yellow, blue, green, black, and white.

PAINTBRUSHES. You will need three good-
quality, sable watercolor brushes in sizes
No. 0, No. 1, and No. 3.

MUFFIN TIN

SMALL STICKS, popsicle sticks, or tongue de-
pressors

METALLIC GOLD LIQUID PAINT, small bottle,
and its proper solvent

CLEAR PLASTIC LACQUER, glossy finish, in an
aerosol can. Use Krylon, Testor's, or some
similar type.

Modeling Clay

The two kinds of modeling material suggested
here are simple to work with and not as messy

as plaster. Both will dry very hard and are easy to paint. You may already be familiar with the materials, since they are commonly used in schools. The grayish, self-hardening modeling clay sold in art-supply stores is of very smooth consistency and is probably the easiest to work with. But it must be bought in five-pound cartons at a cost of about fifty cents per pound—this is rather expensive. Directions for use are given on the package; the clay will stay moist and workable if it is stored in a plastic container with a lid. The cornstarch mixture is also self-hardening, but it is a little more grainy and is apt to crumble if it becomes too dry. Of the two materials, the self-hardening kind dries smoother than the cornstarch mixture and takes color a little better. But the cornstarch clay can be made from ingredients found in most kitchen cupboards, and it is much cheaper than the clay you buy. Here is the recipe:

Ingredients

1 cup salt
1 cup cornstarch

½ cup water
Few drops of cooking oil

Equipment

Measuring cup
Small saucepan
Wooden spoon or
    rubber spatula

Small mixing bowl
Plastic wrap
Pint-sized plastic
    container with lid

52

Measure and mix the salt, cornstarch, and water in the small saucepan. Place the pan over very low heat and cook the mixture from 2 to 3 minutes, or until it becomes stiff, stirring constantly with the wooden spoon or rubber spatula. Remove the pan from the heat and stir in three or four drops of cooking oil. When the material is cool enough to handle, put it into a small mixing bowl and knead it vigorously with both hands, pressing out all the lumps between your thumbs and fingers. Continue kneading until the mixture feels very smooth. If it seems a little stiff and tends to break apart, you can soften it by adding a few drops of water and kneading them into the mixture. Wrap the clay tightly in a piece of plastic wrap and store it in the plastic container with a lid. It will keep almost indefinitely in the refrigerator, but it should always be worked at room temperature.

Both materials will require two days or more to dry in the air if the figures are made no more than $1/2$ inch thick. The cornstarch mixture can be left to dry in the air, or a finished piece can be placed on a cookie sheet and left to bake overnight in an oven set at 250 degrees. When hard, both clays can be smoothed with fine sandpaper if necessary; the cornstarch clay is more apt to need sandpapering.

Before you begin, it is a good idea to experiment with the clay for fifteen minutes or more to see what can be done with it. Cover your work area with wax paper, and start with a hunk of clay the size of a golf ball. Your fingers are the best modeling tools, but any of the simple tools listed will be helpful. Pinch off and roll some bead-sized balls between your palms—see if you can make them all the same size. Make some long "snake" rolls with the palms of your hands. See how thin you can make them before they break. Roll a piece of clay out flat, using the wooden dowel as a rolling pin. Make a pattern of lines on the piece with another tool. Make a small figure of a man and his dog.

Soon you will learn what can and what cannot be done with the material. Clay cannot be worked like wood or stone or metal or wax or anything else; it can only be worked like *clay*, and you will want to learn its possibilities and limitations. After the experiments, work a drop or two of water into whichever kind of clay you are using if it has dried and stiffened a little. Return the clay to the container and put it away until you are ready to make the *santitos*.

Making an Armature

If you have read about making the large *Krampus* in Chapter 2, you already know that in order to construct a free-standing clay figure, you need some kind of stiff skeleton to help hold it up. The first step then is to build an armature, so that the clay will not sag and collapse as it has a way of doing.

First, rule and mark off the cardboard into five pieces $1\frac{1}{2}$ by $2\frac{1}{2}$ inches, which are to be laminated together to make the base. Cardboard has a definite grain to it, and if as you stack up and glue the pieces together, you alternate the direction of the grain, the base will be stronger and less apt to warp. So, measure and mark off the five pieces on the cardboard so that two are going in a vertical direction and three in a horizontal direction. Number the vertical pieces 2 and 4 and the horizontal pieces 1, 3, and 5. Cut them out with the scissors. Using the white glue smoothed on with your finger, paste pieces 2, 3, 4, and 5 together and put them aside to dry under a weight of heavy books or a brick. Draw diagonal lines on piece 1 which will cross at the center point. Punch two small holes with the awl on each side of that point $\frac{3}{4}$ inch apart as shown. This punched piece of cardboard will be the top layer of the base. Do not glue it in place yet.

With the wire-cutting pliers, cut a piece of 18-gauge wire 13 inches long. This wire is to be used to make a vertical armature for the clay figure that will be glued firmly between the cardboard layers of the base.

First shape the wire into a narrow "arch" by bending it in half and pressing the bend together so that the ends are $\frac{3}{4}$ inch apart. Put the two ends of the bent wire through the holes in the cardboard and push the cardboard up on the wire so that it is temporarily out of the way,

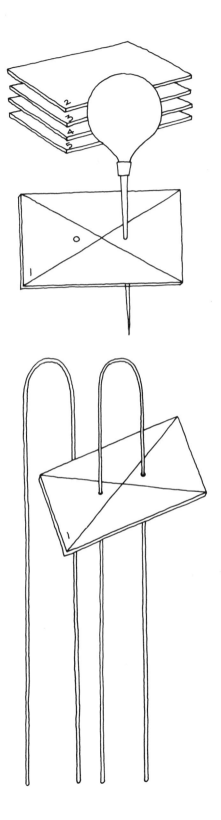

55

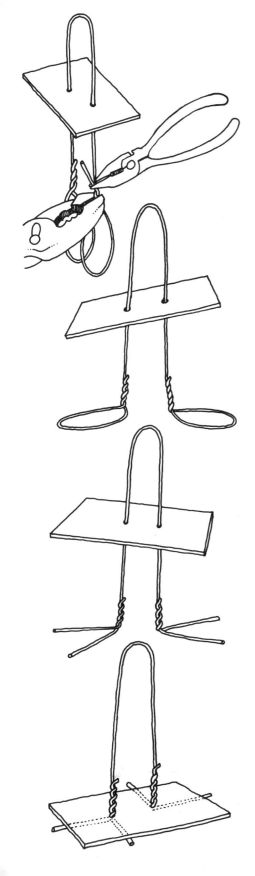

as shown in the drawing. Now, to form the "feet": two inches from one end, bend the wire into a loop with your fingers, so that the end crosses over the main wire and goes about $3/4$ inch past it. Holding the bull-nose pliers in one hand, clamp the wires together firmly at the point where they cross. Use the needle-nose pliers in your other hand to twist the wires tightly together, as in the diagram. Twist three or four times, keeping the bull-nose pliers firmly clamped together around the wires. The loop must be fastened very securely, with the end of the wire wrapped tightly. The trick of bending and twisting wire is always to use *two* pairs of pliers—one to hold the wire and one to twist it. Using the needle-nose pliers, clamp the wire firmly in the center of the twisted section, and with the bull-nose pliers in your other hand, bend the loop out like a flat foot so that it is at a right angle to the main wire. Repeat the operation at the other end of the wire, to form two feet just alike.

Use the wire cutters to clip through the center of each of the loops and straighten out the clipped ends. Spread the four prongs out straight, as shown, and adjust them so that they are at right angles to the "legs."

Push the piece of cardboard down against the bend of the wires (the twisted sections will run up a little way through the holes in the board) and use the pliers to "aim" the ends of the wires toward each of the four sides of the

56

cardboard. Fasten the ends flat against the bottom of the cardboard with masking tape and clip off the wires so that they are even with the edges of the board. Now the long wire arch should stand up straight and firm. Press the bend in the top of the wire together, as it must be narrow enough not to interfere with modeling the neck or head of the figure.

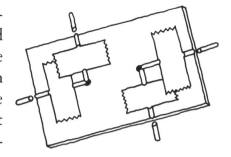

Remove the four glued pieces of cardboard from under the weight and spread glue on top of the stack. Put the piece with the wire armature on top of the others and clamp the stack together with as many spring clothespins as necessary. Set it aside to dry. You will need one armature and base like this for each standing figure. No armature is necessary for the kneeling figure, because it is thicker at the base and is somewhat supported by the wings.

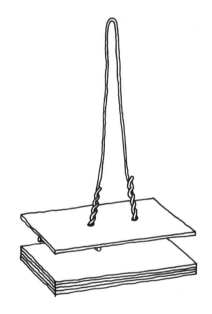

Modeling the Standing Figure

There are no rules for modeling with clay—no right and no wrong way to work. Your own way of shaping, marking, and forming clay is as correct as anyone else's. You are the only person who knows how you want the piece to look—simply make it look the way *you* want it to.

Usually when people work on larger sculptures requiring some sort of support, they model the figure over an armature temporarily

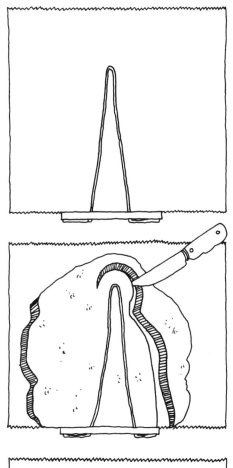

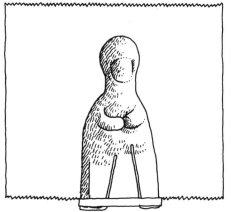

fixed to a platform. The finished piece is then detached from that base, so that a mold can be made from the piece to produce the final casting in plaster, stone, or metal. The finished casting of the sculpture is then sometimes bolted to a new wood or stone base. When you work on small sculptures made of a self-hardening material that require no casting, you can make an armature that is, right from the start, attached to its final base. This is a more logical and simpler way to work.

One easy way to proceed with the clay modeling is to lay the wire armature on a piece of wax paper flat on the edge of your table, with the cardboard base hanging over the table edge. Use the wooden dowel to roll out a piece of clay about $1/16$ inch thick and large enough to form the back of the whole figure. Make a drawing on paper first, if you think it will be helpful. Slip the rolled-out clay under the armature and, with a paring knife, cut out the silhouette of the figure. Press the wire down into the cutout clay a little. With your work in the same position, begin adding clay over the wire so that it sticks to the backing clay, shaping it with your fingers and tools to model the front of the *santito*. The photographs will guide you, or you can use pictures of saints from other books.

You can add clay in the form of rolls, little balls, or roughly pinched-off hunks, then shape and smooth the pieces with a tool or your fingers. Keep a small bowl of water nearby and moisten the material a very little to make the pieces stick together. Don't flood the clay, or the water will have just the opposite effect—things will come apart. These are not rules. They are just hints to help you start working in your own way. Stand the figure up to work on it, if that seems easier to you. Use the tools and your fingers and fingernails to finish the modeling. Use the paring knife to cut away extra clay and note in the photographs that such details as the nose, hands, and the folds of the robe are only barely suggested.

After the piece is finished, you can add a layer of clay to cover the cardboard base if you wish, but do not make it too thin, as the clay is apt to crack; all clay shrinks as it dries. Thin clay cracks, and thick clay caves in a little as it dries; experience will show you what happens. When your piece is finished and absolutely dry, you can smooth it with the fine sandpaper, if you wish, but work gently.

Painting the Santitos

In the Mendivil family of Cuzco, eleven-year-old Hilario and his elder cousin, Maria, do much of the decorating of the plaster *santitos*. Each little figure represents an actual person and wears a distinctively colored robe and sometimes carries certain identifying objects in his hands. Hilario likes to play a joke on his mother, who supervises the painting. There is a native black Peruvian saint named San Martin de Porres, and many of the *santitos* the Mendivils make are of him since he is much revered. Sometimes Hilario paints the face and hands of another figure black, instead of the usual pink used for the white saints, pretending he does not know which saint is which. His mother laughs as she scolds him and throws the *santito* away. The black saint in the photograph is one of Hilario's *wrong* black saints, reluctantly rescued from the waste basket and given to us by Georgina, who would not accept pay for it because it was incorrectly painted.

You can make your *santitos* any color you like. Poster paints are the cheapest and easiest to use and can be bought in sets of six colors in small jars. Sometimes the paints are too thick and need to be thinned with water. A muffin tin with a compartment to hold a little of each color is useful, and six small popsicle sticks to dip paints out of each jar will keep the colors clean. After using a brush in one color, always wash it in clean water before using it in another color.

A good procedure in painting is to apply the lighter colors first—white, pink, and yellow. Then paint the areas of red, blue, or green, and lastly apply the black. Hold the figure by the base as you work and allow each color to dry completely before you paint another color over it or next to it.

Before you paint the face or any detailed designs on clothing, practice painting them on a sheet of scrap paper first. This will give you enough experience so that you won't have to draw pencil guidelines on the figure itself. Look at the faces in the photographs and practice making the eyes and eyebrows with tiny strokes of paint, using the smallest brush you have. The mouth is barely indicated with one light stroke of red; no other details of the face are painted.

When the colors are dry, add a few touches of gold with the smallest brush, after practicing a few strokes on paper. When you have finished, clean the brush in its proper solvent—turpentine or lacquer thinner depending on what the instructions on the label say—and wash the brush with soap and warm water afterward. The gold may take much longer to dry than the poster paints, or it may be quick-drying; check the label. When the gold is dry, paint the base and allow it to dry completely.

To apply the final protective lacquer, work either in a well-ventilated room or out of doors. Stand the figure on a small scrap of cardboard, surrounded by sheets of newspaper. Give the figure three very light coats of spray lacquer, waiting two or three minutes between each coat for the lacquer to dry. Handle only the cardboard to turn the figure so as to spray all sides of it. In Cuzco the *santitos* are painted with a final coat of heavy varnish applied over the colors with a brush, and this dries with a very shiny finish. The spray lacquer is much easier to use, but will not have quite as much shine.

More Decorations You Can Make

When you have begun to learn how to use clay by making a *santito,* you may want to go on and make other small, decorative pieces from this wonderful material. With a few pinches of your thumb and fingers and a couple of pokes with a tool, you can easily make the simple form of an animal or bird, and a little more careful modeling will produce a toy-sized building or a stylized airplane. Thick, solid shapes do not require a supporting armature and are perhaps even easier to make than the Peruvian saints.

Ceramic clays, dug from the earth, have been used for centuries to make useful pots, jars, and plates and also to make toys, ornaments, and figures for special occasions—especially for Christmas. When dried clay pieces are baked in a potter's kiln, the gray earth color changes to dull red, buff, white, or black, depending upon how the heat of the oven affects the various chemicals in the clay. Sometimes the objects are left the soft, natural color and sometimes they are coated with a hard, protective glaze and fired again. Potters in South and Central America and in Mexico like to paint their decorative pieces with bright colors in fanciful designs.

Self-hardening clay has the same plastic quality as potter's clay that has to be fired; it dries very hard but will not be water-resistant. Cornstarch "clay" also dries hard, but is apt to shrink and warp when used for large objects. Both clays are fine for making small, decorative pieces that are to be painted and lacquered like the *santitos*.

The photograph shows a simply modeled small pottery church made in Peru of unglazed

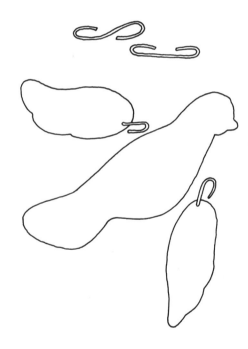

buff clay, fired and freely decorated with water-color paint in two shades of reddish brown. The stylized church is seven inches high and is of a type commonly seen in homes or at primitive roadside shrines accompanied by a few wild flowers in a vase. The Christian Indians of Peru kneel and pray before this miniature symbol of their own parish churches.

Pictured also are a small white and gold clay dove, a blue cat, and a white bell made by village potters in Mexico and decorated with colorful flowers. The ornaments are between 2 and 3 inches tall, and each is topped with an S-shaped wire loop partly embedded in the clay to serve as a hanger for the Christmas tree decoration.

If you make small objects similar to these shown, you can use a typically Mexican way of joining clay pieces together with short lengths of wire. Simply bend the ends of the wire into small loops and embed the ends in the damp clay of the two pieces to be joined. When the clay dries, the wire loops become firmly anchored in it. You can attach wings to birds—like those of the dove in the photo-graph—haloes to angels, and tails to dogs in this way. Colorful painted pottery trees are made in Metepec, Mexico, and leaves, fruit, and birds are stuck on the branches with wires. Mexican potters make no attempt to conceal the wires that may show between pieces of clay, and

64

Clay Christmas-tree ornaments made in Mexico

the method seems to give a rather carefree and amusing style to the finished objects. It also lends a lighter look than if all the joints were solidly make in clay.

The Peruvian saints, the small church, and the Mexican Christmas ornaments will give you ideas for developing your own style of modeled and decorated objects. You can paint your work any color you like—the way Hilario Mendivil *sometimes* does.

The first representation of the Nativity scene in the stable at Bethlehem is said to have been set up in Greccio, Italy, by St. Francis of Assisi. The villagers were much impressed by his presepio *or* crèche. *The custom spread to other communities and is now followed all over the world. Italian cities vie with each other to make the most elaborate and beautiful* presepio.

In Provence, in the south of France, the tiny clay figures used in Christmas crèches are unique in all the world. The small santons, *as they are called, are not dressed in biblical robes but in everyday Provençal clothing, the style of which changes a little each year. Thus an early eighteenth-century crèche reflects in true detail the country-style dress of the period, and the date when the figures were made can be easily identified.*

Between Christmas and New Year's, the streets of Old Poland were lined with beautiful little exhibit stalls called Joselki. *The little booths, which were decorated with tinsel and lighted with candles, contained carefully painted scenes from the Christmas story.*

5
A STAR–TOPPED VIENNESE CANDY TREE

A treeful of sweets and surprises

In this day of dozens of kinds of Christmas-tree ornaments—multicolor glass balls, plastic tinsel, foil icicles, and so on—it may seem hard to believe that you can completely decorate a traditional evergreen tree with one single kind of ornament that you yourself can make and that the tree will be as beautiful as any you have ever seen.

This distinctive kind of tree, which has been familiar for years to the Viennese, is decorated entirely with little candies wrapped in tissue paper and foil in a simple but very ingenious way. The tree is not only pretty, but it represents a charming Old World idea of Christmas hospitality. Every guest or visitor who comes to your home during the several weeks the tree is in place is invited to take a packet from the tree. Instead of having to say, "Don't touch!" you can say to everybody, "Help yourself!" At

67

first the sweets can be replaced by others, though finally by Twelfth Night all the decorations will probably have been eaten!

Viennese families made their own sweets for the tree. The name of the candy is the same in German and in English—fondant. It is a soft, creamy mixture that can be flavored with vanilla, almond, or mint. The semihardened candies are often coated by dipping them into melted chocolate or colored sugar syrup, which hardens when cool. You can find a recipe for fondant in most cookbooks. So that the candy will not stick to the decorative paper, wrap each piece of shaped, hardened fondant in a small square of wax paper. If you don't want to make the candy yourself, you can buy any kind of individually wrapped caramels or hard Christmas candies.

The decorations are made by first rolling up each sweet in a piece of fringed tissue paper, and then wrapping it in silver foil. When the ornamental packets are hung vertically by their green cords on an evergreen tree, they seem to be attached by magic as they flutter and turn like little dancers. These candy packets are the right size to decorate a medium-sized or large standing tree, but they are too large to be used on a table tree.

Until the twentieth century, Christmas trees were lighted by small candles that gave a special sort of glow, but now candles have been replaced almost everywhere by strings of electric lights—which are far safer and very pretty, too. Plain or colored lights and an ornament for the top are the only other decorations the tree will need. If you like, you can make a silver paper star for the top, as described later in this chapter.

Materials and Tools
for the Candy Tree

CHRISTMAS TREE, of course, fixed in its stand, topped with an ornament if you wish, and strung with lights

CANDIES, either homemade or store-bought

WHITE TISSUE PAPER

KITCHEN FOIL, one roll, 12 inches wide

YARDSTICK

PENCIL

SCISSORS

WAX PAPER (if your candies are not already wrapped)

COTTON CORD, green. You can use Coats and Clark's "Speed Cro-Sheen" or any similar cord.

TRANSPARENT TAPE

Wrapping the Candies

The first thing to do is to cut out the pieces of paper to wrap each candy. Lay out flat on the table three full sheets of white tissue paper, placing each one exactly on top of the others and smoothing out any creases. Measure off with the yardstick, mark with the pencil on the top sheet, and cut out with the scissors pieces that measure 7 by 12 inches. Fold each group of three cut pieces in half crosswise, so that your stack of cut pieces measures 6 by 7 inches. Now cut fringe along both 6-inch edges of the stack, holding the tissue paper very tightly together and making the cuts less than $1/4$ inch apart and about 2 inches in length. Separate the three pieces of tissue paper and refold each single sheet on the original fold line. You can, if you choose, wrap some of the candies in bright-colored tissue paper—red, green, or whatever color you like—and some in white, but the more white paper you use, the better.

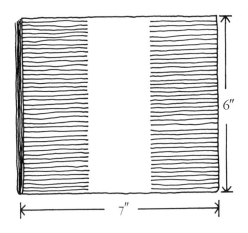

To cut the little pieces of foil, use the metal edge of the box the foil comes in to tear off straight strips $2^{1}/_2$ inches wide. Then with the scissors cut these strips into 4-inch lengths, so that one strip from a 12-inch roll will make three pieces $2^{1}/_2$ by 4 inches.

Cut the green cotton cord into $10^{1}/_2$-inch lengths. Now you have all the materials required to wrap and tie the pieces of candy.

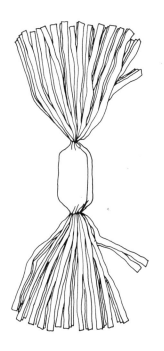

Place one of the candies, wrapped in wax paper, on a piece of tissue paper, centering it on the folded edge, and roll it up tightly. Put the tissue-wrapped candy in the center of the $2^{1}/_2$-inch end of a piece of foil and roll it up tightly. Twist the ends of the foil together by holding the roll in both hands and twisting first one end, then the other to make a tight wrapping. Simple! The foil holds the tissue paper in place, and the twisting of the ends holds the foil. That's all there is to it.

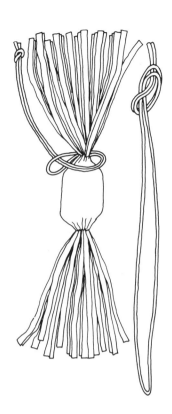

Tie together in a knot the two ends of a 10½-inch length of cord. Place the loop under the "neck" of one end of the wrapped candy, stick the knot through the loop, and pull the hanger up tight. Now the candy is ready to be hung on the tree, and the more pieces you add, the prettier the effect will be. It is hard to imagine, just by reading this description, how elegant the tree will look. And it is nice to know that a candy tree is probably one of the least expensively trimmed trees in the world!

"Überraschung!"

"Surprise!" You can follow a very old Viennese custom that will make the candy tree even more interesting. Buy a few tiny gifts no larger than a piece of candy, wrap them tightly with tissue, and fasten the tissue with transparent tape. Then wrap the little packages again in fringed tissue and foil so that they look exactly like the candy packets. Loop cord around them and hang them on the tree. Inside the ornament they take from the tree, some of your friends will find a surprise gift instead of the piece of candy they were expecting. Here are some suggestions for surprises: any kind of miniature party favor, a pair of earrings, a pin, a key chain, a red eraser, a charm for a bracelet, badges with silly sayings, and other articles you yourself will think of.

Making a Star
to Top the Tree

A silver paper star to go on the top of the tree is as simple to make as the foil-and-tissue candy packets once you have learned the trick of folding the paper. You need only one sheet of paper $8^{1}/_{2}$ by 11 inches—preferably a rather stiff, shiny, silver gift-wrap paper. Four folds and one snip of the scissors will magically produce a star! If the silver paper you want to use seems too flimsy to hold its shape when folded and has a tendency to curl up, you can make it a little

Gold and silver sculptured paper stars

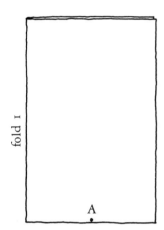

fold 1

A

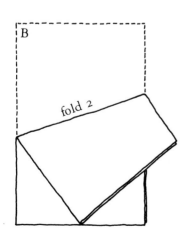

B

fold 2

stiffer by cementing a sheet of plain white bond paper to the back of it before folding it. Coat both sheets with rubber cement, allow the cement to dry, and stick the two sheets together.

The drawings show you exactly how to fold and cut the paper. Follow them carefully.

Materials and Tools for a Sculptured Five-pointed Paper Star

SILVER PAPER, one sheet, $8^1/_2$ by 11 inches

WHITE BOND PAPER and RUBBER CEMENT (optional; to be used if the silver paper is too thin)

RULER

PENCIL

WHITE STRING or heavy white thread, for hanging the star

Place the sheet of paper on the table with the long edge toward you and keep it in that same general position as you fold it.

1. Fold the sheet of paper in half crosswise, so that the silver side is out.

2. With the ruler and pencil measure along the bottom edge $2^3/_4$ inches from the fold and mark a dot, A.

3. Fold the upper left-hand corner of the rectangle (corner B) down at an angle so that it is exactly on dot A. Crease the new fold.

4. Fold the lower left-hand corner (C) up

74

and over the second folded edge so that it fits tightly against it. Crease well.

5. Fold corner D down until the folded edges line up at the left. Crease well.

6. On fold 4, measure down from the sharp point $2^{1}/_{2}$ inches and mark a dot. On the opposite folded edge (fold 3) measure down $4^{5}/_{8}$ inches from the sharp point and mark a dot. With the pencil draw a light line between the two dots; then with one snip of the scissors cut across the folded paper on that line. Discard the piece at the lower right; the sharp point will be at the center of your unfolded star.

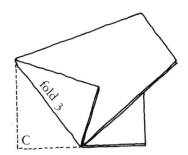

Now unfold the star and reshape it into a three-dimensional sculptured form by reversing the direction of alternate creases. The creases in the center of the points should go upward and those between the points should go downward, like the pleats of an accordion. This will make the center of the star come forward as it hangs on the tree, and the sharper the creases the more depth and dimension your star will have. The star will be about 8 inches across when finished, and this is about right for a tall tree. To make a smaller star for a little tree, fold the same size sheet of silver paper in the same way, and snip it off at the same angle but make the cut closer to the sharp point. To make a larger star, use a larger sheet of silver paper that is in proportion to the $8^{1}/_{2}$- by 11-inch size, for example, 10 by $13^{1}/_{8}$ inches or 12 by $15^{3}/_{4}$ inches. Proceed

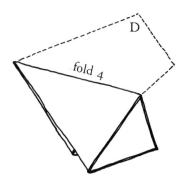

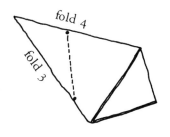

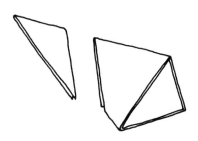

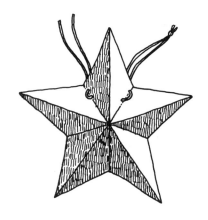

with the folding and cutting in the same way as directed above. Experiment with a sheet of newspaper until you can make the right size star for your tree.

With the point of the scissors, punch small holes in the creases on each side of any one of the star's points. Make two holes on each crease, the first about $1/4$ inch in from the edge, and the second $1/4$ inch below the first, as shown. Put a 10-inch length of white string or thread through each pair of holes, so that the small stitch shows on the front and the ends of the string are at the back of the star. Tie the ends of each string in a knot and use the two knotted cords to tie the star to the topmost branch of the tree.

A tree hung with decorations wrapped only in white tissue paper and silver foil is particularly beautiful, for it looks as if it has been outside in a gentle, fluffy snowfall. If you happen to live where it never snows, or where it is warm at Christmas, the whole tree will be a sort of winterland surprise for everyone who sees it.

Two More Christmas Stars

You can use the same kind of silver paper—or if you like, gold paper of a similar weight—to make a six-pointed sculptured star for the tree. The method is even simpler than the one you used to make the five-pointed star.

76

1. With a pencil compass draw a circle on your paper the size of the outside diameter (width across) of the star you want to make.

2. Cut the circle out with the scissors and fold it in half.

3. Fold the half circle into thirds, with one third turned back and the other third turned forward.

4. Fold the whole wedge-shaped piece in half.

5. Cut across the packet diagonally as shown in the drawing, from the outside corner toward the last fold made.

Unfold the star and reshape it into a three-dimensional sculptured form by reversing the direction of alternate creases as you did on the five-pointed star. The creases in the center of the points should come upward and those between the points should go downward, as in the pleats of an accordion. Attach a hanger in the same way as described for the five-pointed star.

Since stars are used in many decorative ways at Christmas, you may also want to learn how to draw and cut out an ordinary, flat five-pointed star in any size you like. In this way you can make tiny paste-ons for gift packages or a huge star for the window.

Using a pencil compass, draw a circle on lightweight cardboard of whatever size you want. If your compass is small and you want to make a big star, draw around a plate or bowl to

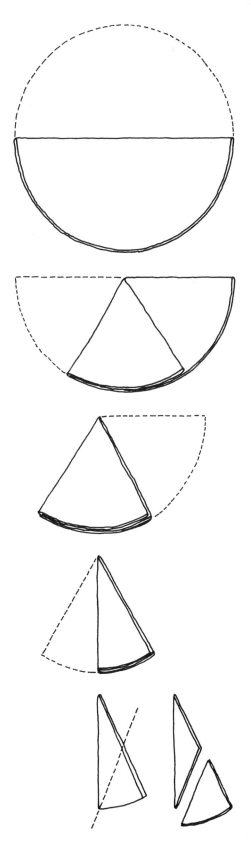

make the circle. The star is to be drawn inside the circle and will therefore look a little smaller than you might expect. Be sure to make the circle large enough. Now look at the drawings and follow these steps:

1. Use a pencil and ruler to draw a horizontal line across the center of the circle, from A to B (through the hole made by the compass).

2. Hold one edge of a stiff, square-cornered card along the horizontal line at the center point, C, and draw the vertical radius of the circle, from C to 2.

3. Find the center of line A–C by measuring with the ruler; mark a small dot at this point, 1.

4. To find point 3, place the point of the compass on 1 and adjust the pencil end so as to draw an arc through point 2 until it hits line C–B.

5. To find point 4, place the point of the compass on 2 and adjust the pencil end so as to draw an arc through point 3 until it hits the outside of the circle.

6. The distance between points 2 and 4 is one fifth of the circumference of the circle. This is the distance between the five points of the star. Leave the compass adjustment as it is and place the point of the compass on 4; then continue to draw the same short arcs around the circumference of the circle marking 5, 6, and 7. The arcs mark the five equally spaced points of the star.

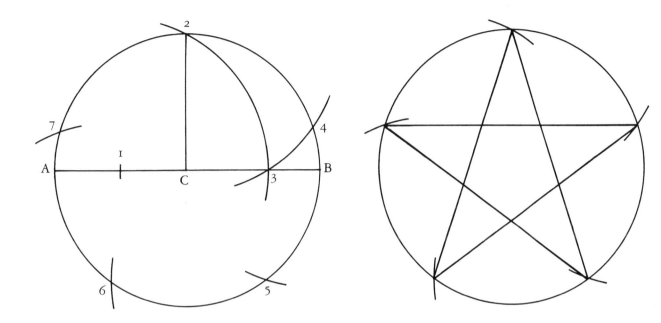

7. Draw straight lines between the five points as shown to make the star.

If this sounds and looks like geometry—well, that's exactly what it is! The procedure looks complicated and sounds worse, but you will soon learn the system and be able to draw stars without even having to look at the diagrams. Cut out your cardboard star with the scissors—cutting from the points toward the center each time. Now you have a neat pattern around which you can draw with the pencil on whatever paper you want to use for the final star. If you make several patterns from small to large in size, you will then be able to cut out stars of whatever size and color you like and scatter them wherever you wish.

The beautiful Christmas carol "Silent Night" was composed in Austria in the year 1818 in the Alpine village of Oberndorf by a music teacher named Franz Gruber. Father Joseph Mohr, a priest, wrote the words.

The Dutch have a humorous custom of giving Christmas gifts they call "surprises." These are presents that are disguised so that they look like something else. For example, a piece of jewelry or a small toy may be concealed in a head of cabbage, in a pudding or a sausage, or even baked in a loaf of bread. Or an inexpensive gift may be put inside a series of larger and larger boxes and finally elaborately wrapped, so that the package looks as if it contains a very important present. Or each of the boxes in the series may have a different name on it, so that the package has to be unwrapped repeatedly and handed around many times before it reaches the recipient.

6
A MEXICAN PIÑATA

A papier-mâché ornament made to be broken

One of the most colorful and joyous customs of the celebration of Christmas in Mexico is the breaking of the piñata. This is a fun-filled and rather explosive game that in some ways resembles what people in the United States call a grab bag. It is used to provide a gay conclusion to a deeply religious Christmas ceremony enacted in every village and city in the land.

The piñata is of Italian origin and is named after the *pignatta,* an ordinary round clay cooking pot. In the early sixteenth century Italian dukes and duchesses amused their guests by staging a game in which such a pot, filled with precious jewels and baubles, was hung from a rope stretched high across the courtyard. Each person was blindfolded in turn and tried to hit the *pignatta* with a long pole. The object of the game was to hit the pot hard enough to break it, whereupon all the titled persons scrambled for the contents.

From Italy the game spread to Spain, and there it began to be played during the Lenten season. The first Sunday in Lent became known

as Piñata Sunday. The word took on Spanish spelling, but it was pronounced in exactly the same way as in Italian. Gradually the plain clay pot began to be ornamented with imported "China" papers and bright streamers, and its round shape was often almost concealed by the decorations.

Then, about 1600, the Spanish colonists who came to the New World brought the piñata to Mexico, along with other new customs, a new language, and a new religion, all of which were eventually adopted by most of the native Indians. Today in Mexico the piñata is used just as it originally was in Spain and Italy, but it has become a part of the celebration of *la Natividad,* the Nativity.

The piñata makes its appearance as a happy finale to the serious Christmas *posadas,* religious festivities, that begin on December sixteenth and are repeated for nine nights until Christmas Eve, or *Nochebuena.* The *posadas* are a reenactment of the search of Mary and Joseph for lodging in Bethlehem. An image of the Christ Child is carried in the procession, and hymns and litanies are sung as the celebrators wind through the streets, carrying lighted candles. In the hill towns of Mexico it is a beautiful ceremony to see. The participants knock on doors and chant a request for a *posada,* or inn, where they may spend the night. Finally, when someone—by prearrangement—agrees to take them in, the procession breaks up and the entertainment begins.

The host of the Christmas party often has a lovely setting for the fun. A rope has been strung between the enclosing garden walls of his home, and attached to it is a hanger that moves along on a pulley. The hanger can be manipulated by the person who holds a controlling cord. The piñata is attached to the hanger where it swings and dances against the starry December sky above the open patio.

A star-shaped Mexican piñata formed around a clay pot and trimmed with foil, ruffled tissue paper, and long paper streamers.

Although the breaking of the piñata is staged mostly for children, adults enjoy it and sometimes play, too. The game begins when the first contestant is blindfolded, whirled around a few times, then is handed a long pole with which to swing at the piñata overhead. Someone holds the rope and keeps the target bobbing out of reach. All the erstwhile singers of the devout religious procession have now become the cheering section for the wielder of the stick. After several wild swings, the batter is out, and the next player is blindfolded and takes a turn. The game goes noisily on until finally someone hits the piñata and breaks it, so that its contents fly down to the ground. Then follows a friendly scuffle to retrieve the scattered treasures, and the pretty piñata has served its purpose.

Mexican children have a simple little song they sing as they play the game:

No quiero oro,	*Don't want gold,*
No quiero plata,	*Don't want silver,*
Yo lo que quiero	*I only want*
Es romper la piñata.	*To break the piñata.*

Professional piñata makers in Mexico, as well as families that construct their own ornaments at home, follow a traditional method. First they encase an ordinary round earthenware pot, called an *olla,* in strips of split cane, tying the strips together in various ways to form a star, a donkey, a bird, or whatever shape the piñata is to be. Then they paste layers of torn newspaper over the cane framework and around the pot, leaving an opening at the top. A sturdy piece of cord is tied around the piñata, with a hanger loop at the top, and colored tissue-paper ruffles, streamers, and other decorations are added. Finally the frilly, decorated piñata is filled with candies, sugarcane sticks, fruits, and other little gifts.

Every village market in Mexico sells the inexpensive pots that are used for cooking as well as for making piñatas. Such pots, however, can

Ollas *in the market at Oaxaca, Mexico.*
The red-clay pots are coated inside with a protective
and rather drippy green glaze.

be found in only a few cities in the United States, so we have devised a very serviceable substitute—an inflated balloon—over which a papier-mâché piñata of true Mexican character can be made. Of course, the prettier your finished ornament is, the harder it may be for you to sacrifice it to someone's well-aimed swat. Maybe you will prefer to keep the brightly colored piñata intact, using it as a hanging decoration in your home, where it will look as distinctive and pretty as almost any Christmas ornament imaginable.

It is surprising what a variety of shapes can be formed over an inflated balloon. You can make piñatas that look like airplanes or clowns, or like fish, elephants, fat-bellied peacocks, and other kinds of animals and birds. The directions that follow are for making a little burro out of cardboard and ruffly, decorated papier-mâché. As you can see in the photographs, the burro piñata is carefully constructed and requires some rather slow and patient work. It is a more ambitious project than some of the others in this book, but if you truly enjoy making things, you may well find that the piñata is your favorite Christmas treasure of all.

A real burro is as typically Mexican as the piñata itself! The big-eared, stubborn little pack animal serves throughout rural Mexico as a combination family pet, work animal, four-legged auto, and small truck. Our piñata will be called

The finished burrito *piñata,*
made by the author

by the affectionate Spanish name *burrito,* meaning simply little burro.

The piñata is made in three stages. First,
you paste strips of newspaper over the inflated
balloon to make the stiff but rather thin papier-
mâché form of the *burrito.* Second, you cut,
shape, and add cardboard pieces for the head,
neck, and legs. (This is easier for beginners than
building a split-cane framework.) Third, you
cut out, and paste to the surface of the papier-

mâché, colorful ruffles of tissue paper that are typical of all Mexican piñatas; then you add the ears and tail and your burro is finished. The materials listed below have therefore been divided into three sections, representing the three stages of construction. The ten or so items required that are not apt to be found in your home are inexpensive to buy.

Materials and Tools for the Piñata

1 . For the Papier-mâché Covering

BALLOON. Use the large, round, stronger kind called "giant" size; usually there are three balloons in a package.

CARPET OR BUTTON THREAD or light string

SCISSORS

FELT PEN, black

NEWSPAPER. You will need about eight or ten full sheets about 23 by 29 inches for making the papier-mâché and a few more sheets to cover your worktable.

WALLPAPER PASTE in powdered form, a small package of about 4 ounces

SMALL BOWL for mixing the paste with water

MEASURING CUP

TEASPOON

TOWELS. You will need a hand towel or large cloth to protect your lap and a bath towel to cradle the piñata.

SPONGE and a dish to hold it

WIRE COAT HANGER

2. For the Burro's Head, Neck, and Legs

CLEAR ACETATE PLASTIC SHEET, about 7 by 9 inches, 3-point weight or heavier. This stiff sheet will protect the book when you are tracing patterns.

MASKING TAPE, $^3/_4$ inches wide

TRANSPARENT TRACING PAPER, three sheets, about 9 by 12 inches

PENCILS, one soft (2B) and one very hard (4H)

RULER

CARDBOARD or bristol board, two pieces, about 9 by 12 inches. It should be white on at least one side, and it must be flexible enough to roll tightly around a tin can or drinking glass without creasing or breaking.

RAZOR BLADE, single-edged

SCISSORS, sharp

HEAVY CARDBOARD or plywood, to protect the table

CARDBOARD TUBES. You will need the cores, measuring about $1^1/_2$ by 11 inches, from two rolls of paper towels.

WHITE BOND PAPER, two sheets, $8^1/_2$ by 11 inches

RUBBER CEMENT, small jar with its own brush in lid

CORD. You will need $3^1/_2$ yards of cotton postal twine, mason's cord, or light jute cord to tie around the piñata and to make a hanger.

3. For Decorating and Finishing the Piñata

TISSUE PAPER. You will need five sheets of good quality white and one each of red, blue, and green (or other colors of your choice). *Important:* Do not use crêpe paper.

YARDSTICK

STRIP OF WOOD or corrugated cardboard. You will need a very thin 13-inch strip made from $3/8$-inch lattice wood, $1/2$-inch half-round molding, or heavy corrugated cardboard cut so that the corrugations run lengthwise.

PARING KNIFE with thin blade

TIN CAN or plastic milk bottle, to use for practice in pasting ruffles

BLACK CONSTRUCTION PAPER, one sheet, about 6 by 9 inches

PENCIL COMPASS (optional)

BLACK PLASTIC TAPE, $3/4$ inch wide

TAILOR'S CHALK, white, to mark dark paper

RED CONSTRUCTION PAPER, one sheet, about 4 by 10 inches

FOIL PAPER in gold or silver. You will need a scrap about 2 inches square for rosettes.

STRAIGHT PINS, two

Making the Papier-mâché Covering

Blow up the balloon until it is about $8^{1}/_{2}$ inches wide by 11 inches long and tie the stretched rubber mouthpiece itself into a knot, or wind heavy thread around it and tie it tight. The balloon should not be blown up to its full size because you do not want it to be round but slightly pear-shaped. With the felt pen, draw two lines around the center of the balloon, one lengthwise and one crosswise, dividing it into four more or less even quarters. At one of the intersections of the lines draw a free-hand circle that measures about three inches in diameter. This is to indicate the top of the burro's back, which is not to be covered with papier-mâché and will serve as the opening of the finished piñata.

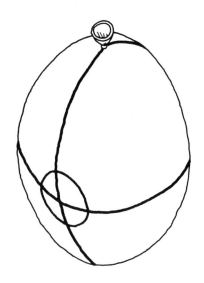

Cover your worktable with newspaper and assemble the materials on the first part of the list. In the small bowl, mix the dry, powdered wallpaper paste with cold water and allow it to stand to thicken according to the directions on the package. For this project about $1^{1}/_{2}$ teaspoons of powder stirred into two full measuring cups of water will make about the right amount of thin, jellylike paste. If the mixture thickens as you work, add more water and stir well.

You will need eight or ten full sheets of newspaper to make the layers of papier-mâché that will cover the balloon and harden to form the piñata. While the wallpaper paste is thickening, tear—do not cut with scissors—the sheets of newspaper into quarters. The uneven edges of the torn strips of newspaper will lie more smoothly against the curved surface of the balloon than the sharp edges of paper cut with scissors.

As you tear, you will discover that there is a definite lengthwise grain to the paper. Tear up each quarter sheet of newspaper along this grain, making strips about an inch wide. They will be about 12 inches long. After a little practice you will find that you can tear two or three sheets at once. Separate the strips and toss them in a heap on the table. If they are in a scrambled pile, you can more easily pick up one strip at a time when your fingers are sticky later.

The balloon is now to be wrapped with four or five layers of paste-soaked strips of newspaper, applied flat like bandage wrappings without folds or twists. First place the strips around the marked 3-inch circular opening, so that you will remember not to cover it. Sit at the table with a protective towel or cloth across your lap, and use it also to wipe your hands when necessary. Dip your fingers into the paste, pull the strip of paper through your fingers until it is coated with paste on both sides, then smooth the wet strip onto the balloon.

Since four or five layers of paper must be applied, you need some way of keeping track of the number of layers. First, cover the surface of the balloon with strips running in a more or less vertical direction, smoothing down each coating as you go. Overlap and slightly crisscross the strips as necessary to cover the balloon surface

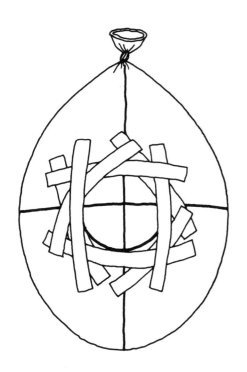

entirely, but do not cover the mouthpiece of the balloon, which is where the tail is later to be attached. Put the balloon down on the folded bath towel to keep it from slithering around, and roll it gently on the towel when you need to blot off excess paste. Use the damp sponge to wipe your fingers whenever they become too gooey.

When the balloon is completely covered, apply the second layer of strips at right angles to the first, in a generally horizontal direction. Alternate the direction of each subsequent layer until you have applied four or preferably five complete coatings. It is better to have too many layers than too few. Admittedly it is difficult to cover a pear-shaped object in such an orderly way that you know exactly how many layers have been applied. Work out your own method of putting on about five layers—that is the important thing.

When you are through, blot off the excess paste on the towel and smooth down the papier-mâché coating with your fingers. Tie one end of a piece of the carpet thread or string to the uncovered mouthpiece of the balloon and attach the other end to a coat hanger. Hang the piñata to dry, preferably in some place that has warm circulating air, such as near a furnace. Although they are not necessary, an electric fan or a hair dryer will speed the drying process. If the piñata is left overnight, it will usually be dry enough for you to continue work in the morn-

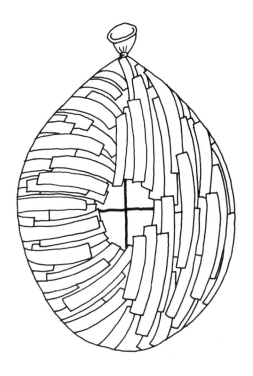

93

ing. When the surface of the paper feels dry to the touch and the papier-mâché has begun to be hard enough so that it will not dent easily, you can proceed. In the meantime, while the paste dries, go on to the second stage in making the *burrito*.

Making and Attaching the Head, Neck, Legs, Tail, and Ears

The patterns in the book for the head, neck, nose cover, legs, hoof covers, tail, and ears are all actual size and are to be traced with transparent tracing paper. Patterns 1 and 2 are two sections of a single piece and are to be drawn on one piece of tracing paper. Tape the left side of the tracing paper to the protective piece of clear plastic and lay these over pattern 1. With the soft pencil, go over all the lines incuding the vertical dotted line labeled "rolling grain of cardboard." (This line is to guide you later in transferring the patterns to cardboard.) Use the ruler as a straight edge when tracing all the straight lines. You need not trace any lettering; you can use the book to guide you later.

Now pull up the first tracing, lay the piece of clear plastic over pattern 2, and tape down the first tracing so that it adjoins pattern 2. The square tabs marked X on patterns 1 and 2

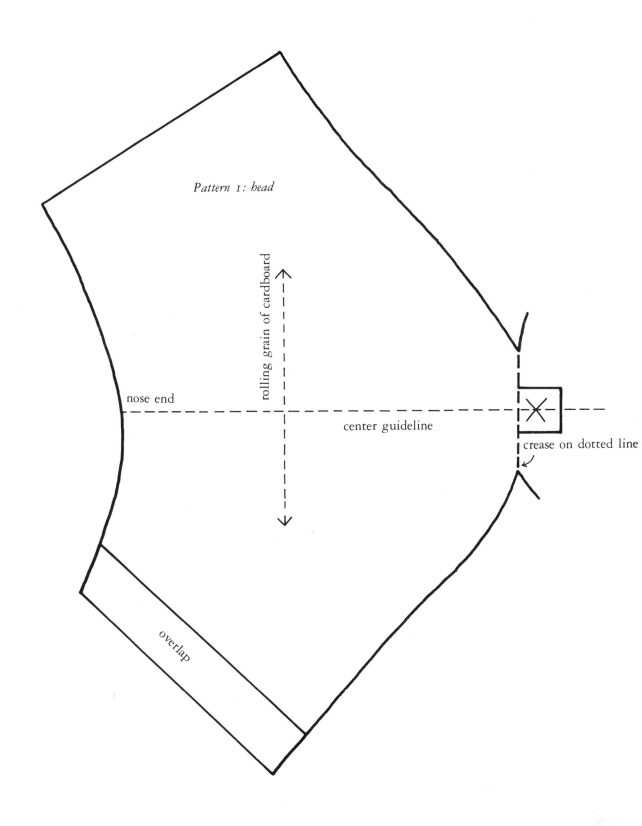

Pattern 1: head

rolling grain of cardboard

nose end

center guideline

crease on dotted line

overlap

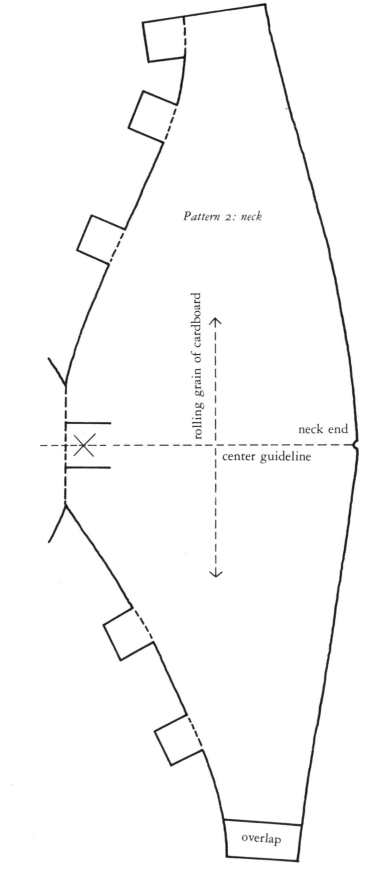

Pattern 2: neck

rolling grain of cardboard

neck end

center guideline

overlap

should be exactly on top of each other. Again trace all the lines, including the "rolling grain" guideline, and ignore the lettering.

Trace patterns 3, 4, 5, 6, and 7 in the same way. Remember to use a ruler to help you trace the straight lines.

Turn all the tracings over and on the back, go over the lines, pressing heavily with the soft pencil so as to blacken them. This is the way all professional artists prepare their tracings—they never use carbon paper because it is apt to smudge. When all the lines on the back of the patterns have been blackened, you are ready to transfer the patterns to the white side of the cardboard or to the bristol board. With masking tape, fasten each tracing in turn to the cardboard, making sure that the dotted arrows follow the rolling grain of the cardboard. Cardboard has an even more decided grain than newspaper and simply cannot be rolled or bent *against* the grain. Just roll the cardboard in your hands, and you will easily discover the grain.

Use the hard pencil to redraw all the traced lines to transfer them to the cardboard. Note that you need only *one* cardboard copy of patterns 1, 2, 3, 4, and 6, but *four* copies of pattern 5 for the hooves, and *two* of pattern 7 for the ears. Blacken the lines again on the back of the tracing paper after making each copy in preparation for the next transfer.

Cut out all the cardboard pieces very carefully and accurately with sharp scissors. On the

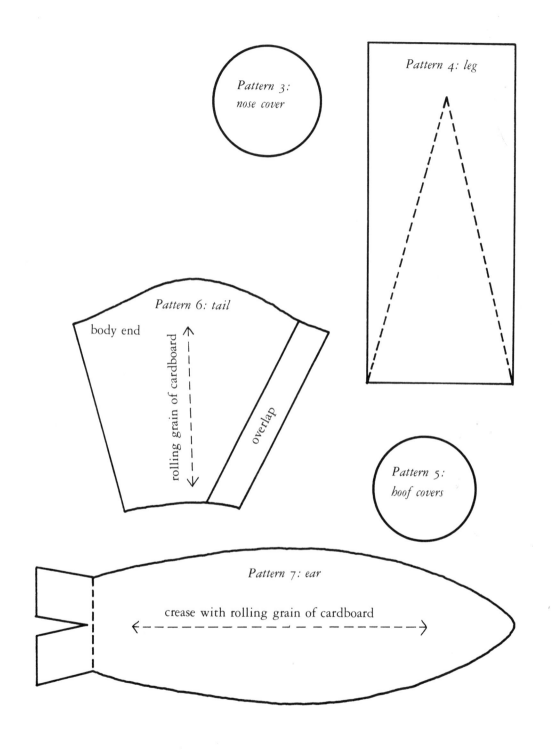

Pattern 3:
nose cover

Pattern 4: leg

Pattern 6: tail

body end

rolling grain of cardboard

overlap

Pattern 5:
hoof covers

Pattern 7: ear

crease with rolling grain of cardboard

copy of pattern 2, use a single-edged razor blade to cut out the hard-to-reach areas between the little square tabs. Put a piece of heavy cardboard or plywood on your table to protect the surface from razor cuts.

The legs are to be made from sections of paper-towel tubes. Use the ruler and pencil to mark off the two cardboard tubes into four $3^{1}/_{2}$-inch lengths. With the pencil draw lines straight around each tube as guides for cutting them; then cut the sections with the razor blade, using a sawing stroke. Hold the small triangular pattern 4 against the base of each leg section and draw around it with the soft pencil. Cut out the triangular sections with scissors and discard them.

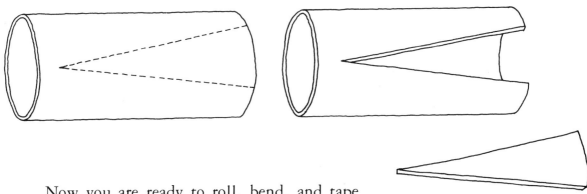

Now you are ready to roll, bend, and tape together with masking tape all the cardboard pieces for the head, neck, legs, tail, and ears. Begin with the pieces cut from patterns 1 and 2. Handle them carefully and with the white side out roll each of them—first pattern 1, then

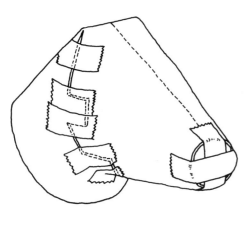

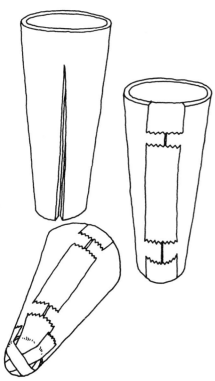

pattern 2—into a slightly rounded shape. Tape each piece together separately at the end marked "overlap." Fasten these ends very accurately and firmly together exactly on the lines; otherwise, none of the pieces will fit. Following the diagram, crease the head across the top along the dotted line on the pattern labeled "crease on dotted line." Join the head and neck, taping them together firmly with all the tabs taped flat against the *outside* of the head section. Tape on the nose cover (pattern 3) with two narrow criss-crossed pieces of tape, about 3 inches long. Now you can see that this section has taken shape and is ready to be attached to the body. It may look a little skinny, but the tissue paper ruffles will fatten it up quite a lot. Lay the pieces aside temporarily.

Close up each of the leg sections by taping together the cut edges of the triangular spaces. Look at the drawing, and you will see that the edges just meet; they do not overlap. Use enough masking tape to fasten the edges together very firmly. Then put each of the circular hoof covers (pattern 5) over the small end of a leg and tape it in place with two narrow pieces of tape, about $2^3/4$ inches long. Roll up the tapered tail piece (pattern 6), white side out, hold it tightly so that the edge is lined up accurately against the overlap mark, and fasten down the edge with tape. Crease the ears slightly down the center. If your cardboard is not white on both sides, cut out two pieces of plain white paper from pattern 7 and paste them on the gray side of the ears. Coat both paper and cardboard with rubber cement, allow it to dry, and press the paper in place. Lay the ears and tail aside.

When you think the papier-mâché of the body has dried enough to be handled, press a piece of masking tape on the surface, and if it sticks, you can proceed. If not, give the piece a little more time to dry. Leave the balloon intact—it will continue to provide a firm surface to work on.

Before attaching the neck and legs, it is necessary to tie a cord around the piñata to make a secure hanger for it. With the felt pen, draw guidelines going in three directions all the way around the body, as shown in the drawing. The cord is to follow these lines. Wrap the cord around the body, as if you were tying up a package, and knot it securely. Then at the top of the body tie a loop about 3 inches in length. The loop should be attached over the opening and just slightly ahead of the center of it. Now cut a number of $1^1/_2$-inch lengths of masking tape, and so that the cord cannot possibly slip, tape the cord to the body around the opening and near the crossing places of the cord. The tissue-paper decorations will hide the cord and other construction details—everything except the hanger loop, of course.

Now you are ready to attach the neck and legs to the *burrito*'s fat body. The places where

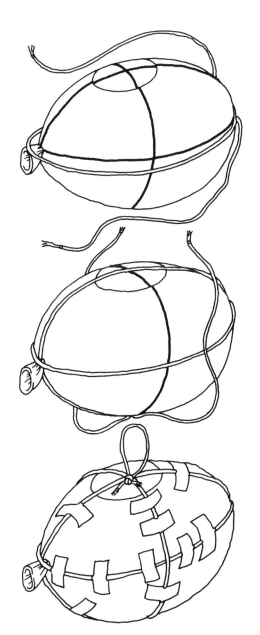

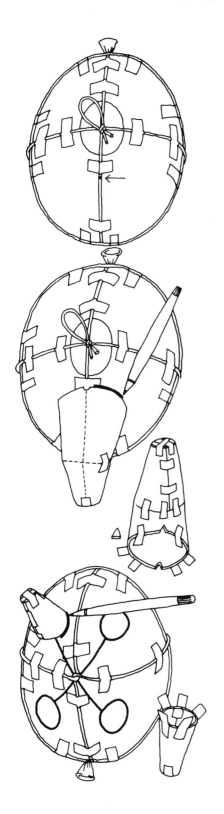

the base of the neck and tops of the legs will be attached are to be outlined with the felt pen. To figure out where to put the neck, measure forward (toward the more rounded or head end of the body) 4 inches from the point where the two cords cross in the center of the opening. Mark the point clearly with the felt-tipped pen. It is the spot where the center top of the neck is to go. The tiny notch at the top of the neck on pattern 2 fits over the wrapping cord. Hold the neck temporarily in place, matching the center guideline to the point you just made on the body and with the felt pen draw a circle around the base of the neck. Mark on the lower edge of the neck the spot where the cord is, remove the piece, and cut a small notch with the razor blade to fit over the cord.

To mark the places where the legs are to be attached, turn the body of the piñata upside down. With the ruler and felt pen, draw two diagonal lines that cross at the point where the cords cross. Extend the lines about $4^1/2$ inches from the center point where the cords cross. Draw around each leg.

Cut up a good supply of 2-inch lengths of masking tape, and cut them in half lengthwise. Stick the strips temporarily along the edge of your worktable where they will be handy. Use these narrow tabs to attach the neck and legs to the body as shown in the photograph. Press half of each tape on the part to be attached, hold the neck and each leg in turn on the

102

The half-finished piñata,
ready to be covered with
tissue-paper ruffles

marked circle, and press the other half of the
strip of tape firmly on the body. Use plenty of
strips and position them as shown in the photograph. Place all four legs so that the seams are
toward the tail end of the burro. If the neck or
legs can be wiggled at all after taping, apply
more strips of tapes, pressing them flat against
the body over the joints of the first tapes.
Whenever you must put the piñata down, put it

carefully on its side on the bath towel, which you have bunched up, to keep it from rolling.

The ears and tail are small and fragile, so they should not be attached until later when most of the tissue-paper frills have been applied. Handle your *burrito* with tender care from now on, and hold it over the table whenever you are working on it. A fall to the floor at this point might prove fatal, before the piñata's time has come.

Decorating and Finishing the Piñata

The *burrito*'s body—all except the ears, tail, and legs—is to be covered solidly with rows of small tissue-paper ruffles. The ruffles are made by a simple method of cutting, folding, and pasting thin tissue paper. All Mexican piñatas have frilly surfaces made in this way; even though sometimes the decorations may seem rather inappropriate—on such objects as a burro, a fish, or a star—they are, nevertheless, appropriate on a truly Mexican piñata!

If you use the tissue-paper colors suggested (see those listed earlier in the chapter under the heading "Decorating and Finishing Your Piñata"), your *burrito* will have a body of white tissue-paper ruffles with a blue mane and tail fringe, a bright red-and-green striped blanket across his back, and a red halter. White and bright colors are always used on piñatas, but

104

you may choose another color scheme if you wish. It is best to avoid brown, gray, black, or other drab hues.

All the paper ruffles are to be cut out, folded, cut again, then pasted with quick-drying rubber cement according to the simple directions and diagrams. Rubber cement works differently from other kinds of glue and paste; it must be brushed thinly on *both* surfaces to be joined and allowed to dry. The instant those dry cemented surfaces are put together, they stick permanently and cannot be moved around or changed. Do not try to make your piñata with any other kind of paste or glue, or you will have an awful mess.

To make the ruffled strips, start with five sheets of the white tissue paper—or whatever color paper you have chosen to cover the body—and stack them up so that their edges are even. Measure, rule off with the yardstick, and mark with the pencil on the top sheet six or seven strips running across the width of the sheets. The strips should be $2^1/_2$ inches wide and about 20 inches long. Hold the sheets tightly together and cut off the rows of strips, then cut each stack of strips in half crosswise, so that your pieces are about 10 inches long. (A 10-inch strip is about the right length to handle easily when you rubber-cement.) Put the five-layered stacks of strips crisscrossed in a pile, so that they can be easily picked up and cut again, five layers at a time.

Fold each stack in half lengthwise and crease

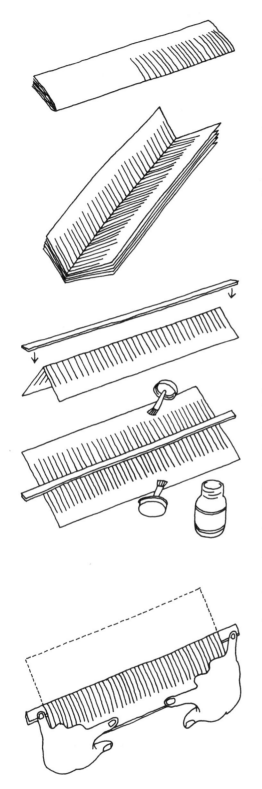

the fold well. Starting at the folded edge, cut straight into the stack toward the opposite edge, but stop the cuts about $3/8$ inch from that edge. Keep making the shallow cuts about $3/8$ inch apart all the way along the folded strip. It is not necessary to draw guidelines for these cuts.

Fold and cut each stack of strips in the same way. Take time to cut the strips carefully and uniformly—it will make a difference in the way the finished piñata looks.

After you have cut all the strips, open out the stack and gently pull off the innermost strip. Lay it on a piece of newspaper with the crease up, standing like a tiny, long tent, then put the 13-inch strip of thin wood or corrugated cardboard on the fold to flatten the piece, as shown in the drawing. Hold the strip of wood down tight and brush rubber cement lightly on the two lengthwise edges of the weighted strip of paper. Let the rubber cement dry for a few seconds, then holding the stick in place with your little fingers, fold the piece up over the stick and join the two edges. Press them together. By folding the strip in the opposite way from which it was folded when cut, you make the strip tubular in shape and the loops of the ruffles nicely rounded.

The rubber-cementing will take some practice, but it is not difficult. Remember to hold the stick down firmly when working and leave it inside the tube. After the two edges have

106

been coated and pressed together, spread rubber cement on the upper side of the two-layered edge, and when it has dried, remove the stick. The piece is now ready to be applied to the body of the burro.

It is a good idea to cut up newspaper into small pieces measuring about 6 by 12 inches, and to use a fresh piece to lay the tissue on *every* time you apply the rubber cement. Discard the newspaper pieces after each strip has been coated. If the edge of the coated tissue strip is hard to pick up, hold the the stick down and loosen the tissue paper by running the blade of the thin-bladed paring knife under it.

Now the tubular ruffles with cement on the straight edges are ready to be applied to the piñata. Each row of ruffles is to be stuck on a little less than half an inch below the previous row. The strips must all head in the same direction, so that each new row of ruffles will cover the edge of the row applied above it.

Before you start decorating the *burrito,* practice pasting about four strips of prepared ruffles around a tin can or plastic milk bottle. Brush a coat of rubber cement in a narrow strip straight around the can or bottle and allow it to dry. Paste the rubber-cement-coated edge of the first row of ruffles straight around the can with the ruffles facing up and the edges down. Apply cement lightly to the edge of this first ruffle, allow it to dry, then stick on a second, a third, and a fourth row in the same way, cementing as

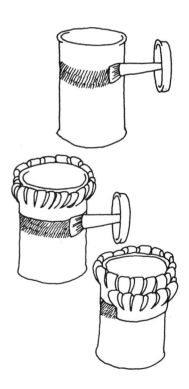

107

you go. The rows should be about $^3/_8$ of an inch apart and all headed in the same direction. This bit of practice will show you how to space the rows evenly and how very little rubber cement is needed to hold them. Fortunately the strips of ruffles can be pieced. The spot where you have to add a new strip to fill out a long row won't show at all. If necessary, you can even paste on a scrap of ruffle so small that it has only two loops. This makes it easy to work around the burro's ears, legs, and tail, by using the right-sized sections of ruffles as little patches. The tissue strips can also be directed into slight curves, but make sure that the ruffles always head in the same direction—once you have started—with one exception, which will be explained later.

Before applying the ruffles to the piñata, use the felt pen to draw guidelines for the "blanket" area on the *burrito*'s back. It is centered over the opening and should measure about 6 inches from front to back, and come down to about the line of the cords on the sides of the body. Also draw guidelines in a generally vertical direction around the body about $1^1/_2$ inches apart. These will help you to apply the ruffles in orderly rows.

If the balloon is still intact, you should now puncture and remove it. You may be surprised to find how hard and rigid the five-layered papier-mâché body has become. But don't bang it against anything or drop it!

Mexican artisans usually work with the

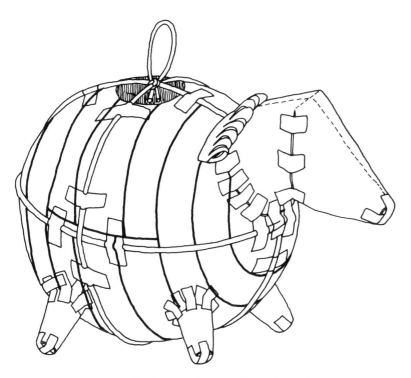

piñata suspended from the ceiling by three or four cords that serve to hold the piece more or less still during the ruffle-adding process. The worker stands and simply moves around the piñata. This is not a bad idea, but if you cannot devise a way to do it, try not to handle the piñata any more than is necessary as you work because the ruffles are easily flattened and crushed. Use the cord hanger as a handle to pick up the piece, and work with the *burrito* standing on his feet as much as possible.

Start by pasting white ruffles on the top of the body at the point where the neck and body join. The loops should face forward, toward the head, and the edges back, toward the tail. Remember that you must spread rubber cement lightly on the edge of each strip of ruffles and

109

also on the papier-mâché body, row by row, as you proceed; both coats of cement must be dry. Follow the guidelines, applying the ruffles all the way around the body, until you come to the marked-off blanket area. Fill that area with about four rows of red ruffles, then three rows of green, then four more of red—or follow this same general plan in applying whatever other colors you may have chosen to use. Continue to work in the same direction as you did when adding the white strips, skipping the hole, of course. Snip off the ends of the strips as necessary to keep the lower edges of the blanket straight.

When adding the rows of white ruffles to the belly side of the *burrito,* put the piñata down on the bunched-up bath towel rather than directly on the table. Or you can use the crumpled bath towel to line a large mixing bowl and cradle the burro in that. Continue applying tissue strips around the body until you are about 2 inches from the tail. After the piñata is finished, if some of the ruffles have become flattened, you can run a pencil through the tissue-paper loops and restore them by pulling very gently.

Apply ruffles very close to the tops of the legs, allowing the edges of the last row to extend down the legs about $3/4$ of an inch. Because legs would look too fat if ruffles were applied to them, they are to be covered with

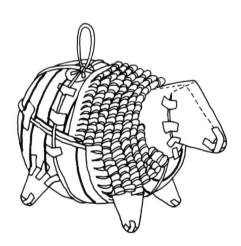

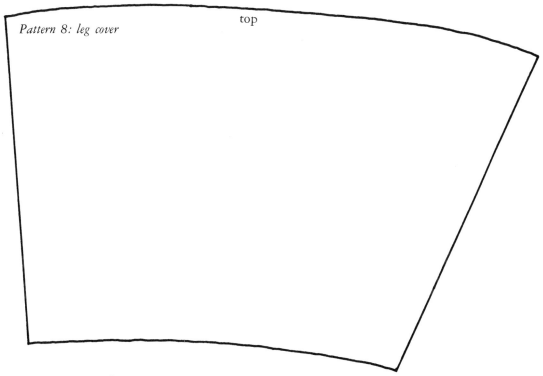

Pattern 8: leg cover

top

paper. To make these covers, trace pattern 8 four times on plain white bond paper and cut out the pieces. Apply a thin coat of rubber cement to the entire back of each piece of paper and also to the surfaces of all the legs. Fit the covers around the legs with the seams facing the *burrito*'s body. Be sure to conceal the raw edges of the rows of ruffles at the tops of the legs. After each cover is in place, apply rubber cement to both surfaces of the overlap and press them well together. Trim the ends if necessary.

To finish the hooves, trace pattern 5 four times on black construction paper, or use a compass to make circles of the right size. Cut

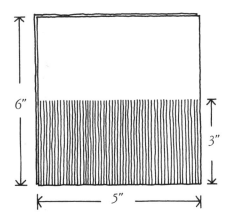

6"

5"

3"

out the circles. Put rubber cement on the back of all four cutouts and on the bottoms of the four hooves. When the cement is dry, paste the black hoof covers on. Now cut two pieces of black plastic tape, $4^1/4$ inches long. Cut them in half lengthwise and wrap a strip around the bottom of each leg.

The white cardboard tail is to have a fringe of blue tissue paper coming out of the small end of it. Cut two pieces of blue tissue paper 5 by 6 inches. Use the white tailor's chalk to mark guidelines for cutting. Hold the two pieces together and cut into one 5-inch edge to make "fringing" cuts very close together and about 3 inches deep. Hold the two fringed pieces together and roll them up tightly with the fringe at one end. Stick the roll into the small end of the cardboard tail and secure it inside with masking tape as shown in the drawing. Fit the tail over the place where the mouthpiece of the balloon was, with the fringe pointing down. Mark the spots where the cord touches the edges of the tail and cut out two notches. Attach the tail to the body with masking tape.

Finish adding the white ruffles to the body, bringing the last strips together around the tail and against it. Now the tail must be covered with white bond paper. Use pattern 6 to draw the cover, cut it out, and after applying rubber cement, put it carefully on the tail with the seam underneath.

Begin covering the head by attaching the

blue ruffles for the mane and forelock. These strips need to be cut a little wider than the others, so that the mane will stand up a little higher than the surrounding white covering. Use the yardstick and white tailor's chalk to measure and mark off two strips 10 inches long and 3 inches wide, using two sheets of blue tissue paper. Cut the strips, fold, cut, and rubber-cement the edges together around the stick in the same way you did before. The mane runs straight down the center of the back of the neck and is made from four strips of ruffles cut three inches long. Apply two strips of blue ruffles with the edges pointing down the *left* side of the burro's neck, and two rows with edges pointing down the *right* side. The ruffles should meet very closely in the center. The mane should just fill the space between the body and the top of the head.

The forelock is made of three strips of blue ruffles cut two inches long and applied perpendicular to the mane. The strips should touch the mane and should be centered across the top of the head, with the loops pointing toward the tail and the edges pointing toward the nose.

The rest of the neck and head should be covered with white ruffles, with the loops pointing toward the body and tail and the edges pointing toward the nose—in other words, in the opposite direction from the ruffles on the body. The new rows at the base of the neck should start right against the first row on the body. Draw

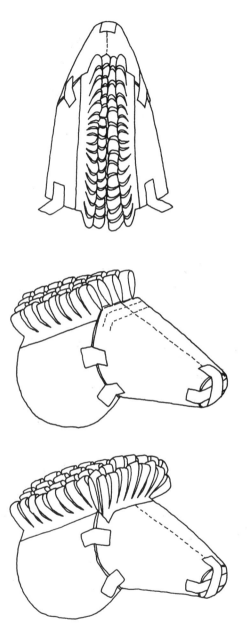

113

guidelines around the neck and head as shown in the drawing.

Attach about four white strips of ruffles around the neck, or up to within an inch of the top of the head. Stop here and at this point attach the ears. Brush rubber cement on the underside of the two creased attachment tabs on each ear, and also on the head itself. When the cement is dry, press the ears in place, but look at the photograph of the finished piñata to help you in placing them. Look at your *burrito* from both sides and front to be sure the ears match and point forward in a cocky position. To secure the ears, press on small tabs of masking tape over the tabs. Now continue covering the head with white ruffles, filling in closely around the ears and up against the mane and forelock, finishing at the tip of the nose.

Use pattern 3 again to draw and cut out a nose cover from the red construction paper. Paste it over the cardboard nose cover. Cut a strip of red construction paper $3/8$ inch wide and 5 inches long and paste it around the end of the nose. Rubber-cement the ends firmly together.

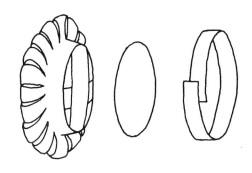

Trace the two eyes from pattern 9 on black construction paper, cut them out, and coat the opposite sides of the two eyes with rubber cement, in order to make a right and left eye with the more pointed corner toward the center of the nose. Look at the photograph again to use it as a guide in placing the eyes. On the spots where the eyes go, smash down the ruffles with your fingers and apply rubber cement generously. Press on the eyes.

Pattern 9: eye

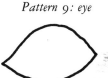

To make the *burrito*'s halter, cut from red construction paper one strip $3/8$ inch wide by 3 inches long for the noseband and another $3/8$ inch wide by $9^{1/2}$ inches long for the headpiece. Coat the noseband on the back with rubber cement and apply a strip of cement also around the top of the *burrito*'s nose, between the second

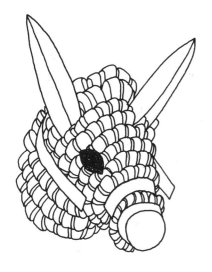

Pattern 10: rosette

and third rows of ruffles. Press the noseband into place.

Put rubber cement on the ends of the pasted-down noseband and on both sides of both ends of the headband. Put the headband around the *burrito*'s head, starting in the center just behind the ears, and bring the ends down to meet the ends of the noseband. Press the ends together. Do not try to pull the headband tight.

Now use pattern 10 to trace and cut out two little rosette fasteners for the points where the halter strips meet. Use the scrap of gold or silver paper. Coat the backs of the rosettes with rubber cement and press them in place. Stick a round-headed pin straight through the rosettes and cardboard into the hollow head to help hold the rosettes in place.

At last your roly-poly little *burrito* is finished and ready to be filled with sweets and small gifts if he is to be a target for your friends at a Christmas piñata party, or hung up where he can be admired as a holiday decoration and work of art.

Beginning on Christmas night, and continuing for two weeks, groups of Romanian boys go about singing carols and reciting poems called colinda. *The choirboys carry with them on a long pole a* Steauo, *a wooden star that is decorated with little bells and colored paper and that bears a picture of the Holy Family, lighted by a candle.*

116

7
MORAVIAN CHRISTMAS COOKIES

*How to form your
own cutters and
make decorative cookies*

Moravia is a small region in central Europe with a name so pretty that it sounds like a fairy-tale kingdom. But it is indeed a very real place with a history that began in the sixth century. However, Moravia has been an independent kingdom with its own ruler for only thirty-five years of its fourteen centuries of existence! Its larger neighbors have controlled Moravia's destiny, so that over the years it has been a protectorate, a crown land, and a province of six other nations. It is now a part of Czechoslovakia.

Throughout the centuries the Moravian people have proudly preserved their Slavic heritage and their strongly united church, the Moravian Brethren. The people do not consider themselves to be German, Austrian, Hungarian, Polish, Bohemian, or Czech, although at times their land has been a part of all those countries.

It was in 1740 that the first Moravians came to America and settled in the area that is now Pennsylvania, where they acquired five thousand

acres of land along the Delaware River. The people were devoutly religious and Moravians were unique among eighteenth century colonists in that many of them belonged to the titled aristocracy of Europe. They founded several communities to which they gave New Testament names, like Bethlehem and Nazareth. Two of their settlements—one in Bethlehem, Pennsylvania, and another in Winston-Salem, North Carolina—are still the centers of Moravian life in the United States.

The American Moravians have preserved many of their traditions, especially their Christmas customs, some of which are unusual and beautiful. Before Christmas, the women of the Moravian Brethren make beeswax candles by the hundreds with decorative folded paper holders attached to the bases. At Christmas Eve services, every member of the congregation holds a flaming candle in his or her hands. The service ends with the singing of a beautiful hymn during which the candles are lifted and held high in the air.

Moravians are excellent cooks, and their small cakes and tarts called *gëback* are famous. These baked delicacies include cookies that are traditionally used to decorate the Christmas tree or hang in windows during the holidays. The cookies are made according to an established rule that is adhered to in every family. Two kinds of cookies are baked: one from a very light-colored dough; the other from a dark,

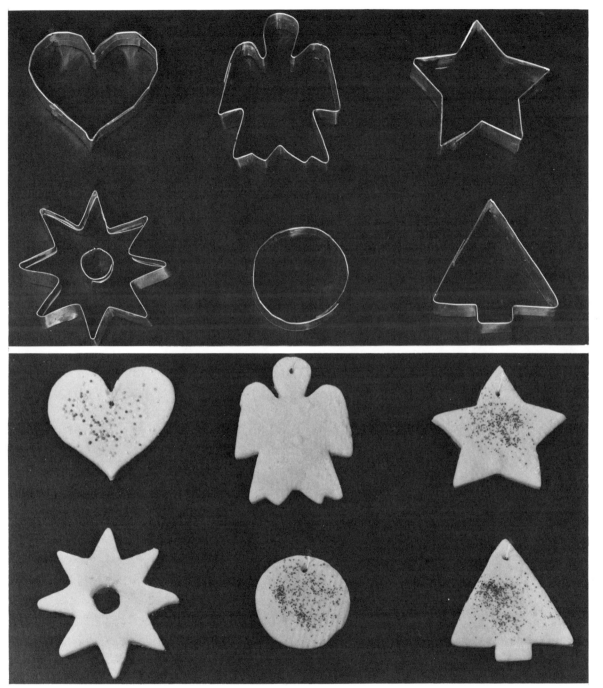

Cutters for the light-colored vanilla cookies, and the baked and decorated cookies.

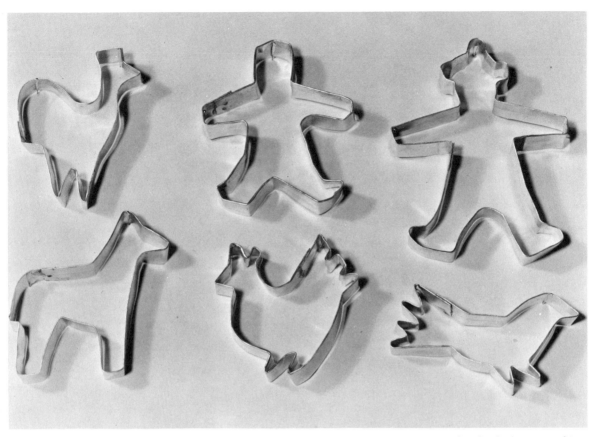

Cutters for the dark spice cookies,
and the baked cookies decorated with sugar, raisins,
and designs made with a toothpick

spicy dough. They are cut out with fancy metal cutters, but only certain shapes are used for the light-colored cookies, and only certain others for the dark ones. The light cookies are cut in the shape of stars, angels, hearts, trees, and flowers; the dark ones in the shape of men, roosters, birds, and other animals.

Anyone who has not seen an evergreen tree ornamented with fancy cookies and only a few

other bright ornaments can hardly imagine how pretty such a tree can be. Cookies are not only decorative but also a symbol of hospitality. Edible stars, roosters, horses, gingerbread boys, angels, and birds decorating the tree, and a big jar full of cookies nearby, ready to replace whatever is eaten, and cookies hanging in the windows of your home, saying, "Come in. Have one"—what a happy idea!

You probably cannot buy commercial cookie cutters in all the shapes mentioned above, but you can make your own cutters from strips of shiny sheet aluminum, to form the twelve designs shown in the photographs. And you can devise even more shapes of your own, once you have learned how the cutters are made. At the end of this chapter you will find two authentic Moravian recipes—one for the light and one for the dark cookies.

Materials and Tools
for the Cookie Cutters

ALUMINUM FLASHING, .016 gauge. You will need one piece 9 inches wide by 30 inches long to make thirteen cookie cutters. The width and length of the pieces of metal required to make the cutters are given on the layout on page 128. If you choose to make only a few of them, you can find the dimensions for making each cutter on the pattern itself, labeled "star," "horse," "tree," etc. Aluminum flashing is an inexpensive, light, flexible sheet metal. The kind suggested here is used in making roof joints and is sold in builders' supply and hardware stores. It comes in long, shiny rolls that range from 6 to 10 inches in width and can be bought by the running foot. It is a good idea to buy a little extra metal in order to have enough to practice cutting and bending it.

CLEAR ACETATE PLASTIC SHEET, about 7 by 9 inches, 3-point weight or heavier. This stiff sheet will protect the book when you are tracing patterns.

MASKING TAPE or transparent tape, $1/2$ inch wide

TRANSPARENT TRACING PAPER, two or three sheets, about 8 by 10 inches

FELT PEN, black with fine point

SCISSORS

RULER, metal, or wooden with a good metal edge. (A plastic ruler will not work.)

AWL

TIN SNIPS, heavy-duty with straight blades

CAST-IRON VISE (essential)

CLAW HAMMER. The small, half-pound size will be easier to use than a full-size carpenter's hammer.

WHITE PAPER, two or three sheets, about 7 by 9 inches

PLYWOOD. You will need a piece $3/4$ inch thick and at least 6 by 8 inches.

FINISHING NAILS, about twenty-five, $1 1/2$-inch 3-penny nails

SMALL WOOD BOARD, $3/4$ inch by 2 by 6 inches

BULL-NOSE PLIERS

NEEDLE-NOSE PLIERS

WOODEN DOWEL ROD, piece $3/8$ inch in diameter and 4 or 5 inches in length

EPOXY GLUE, in a set of two tubes or containers

PLASTIC WRAP kitchen paper

CLOTHESPINS, six or eight, spring-clip type

Cutting Out
the Patterns

The Christmas-tree cookie cutter is the easiest to make, and the star is the next easiest, because straight sides are simpler to form than curved ones. So it is best to start with one of these patterns in order to gain a little experience in shaping the aluminum.

To trace any of the cookie-cutter patterns, put the sheet of clear plastic over the book page and tape a sheet of tracing paper to it. Trace the outlines of the cutter very slowly and carefully with the black felt pen. Trace the heavy black dots on each pattern—these show where the nails will go. Trace also the small arrow marked "start." You need not trace the little circle near the top of each pattern. It shows where to put a hole in the cookie if you plan to hang it up as a decoration. If you are tracing more than one pattern, pull up the tape and move the tracing paper so as to leave at least an inch of space all around each design. Three or four patterns on one sheet of tracing paper will leave you about the right amount of room.

With the scissors cut out the patterns about 1/2 inch *outside* the traced lines and lay the tracings aside.

Now mark off the dimensions of the pattern strips on the piece of aluminum, using the ruler and the felt pen. The dimensions for each de-

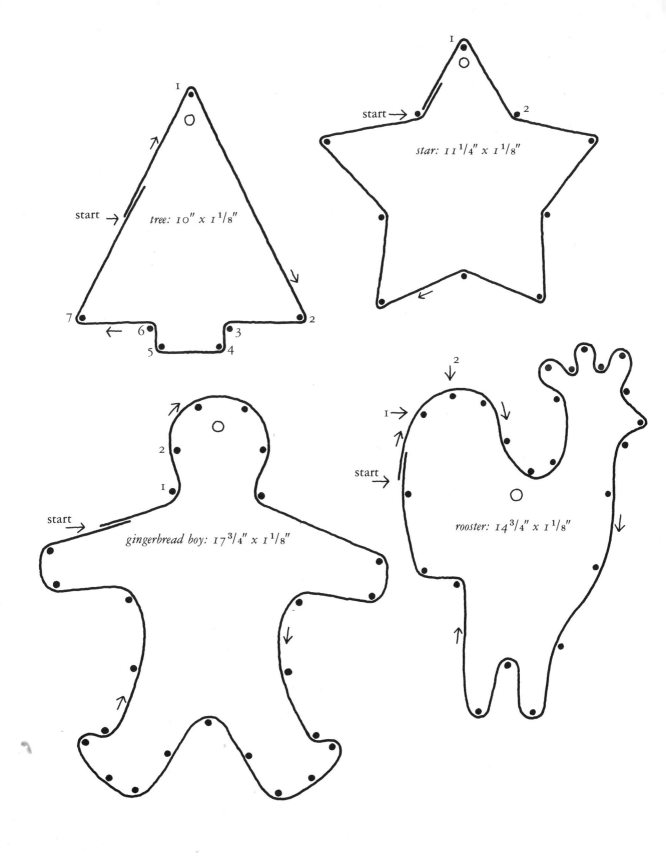

tree: 10" x 1 1/8"

star: 11 1/4" x 1 1/8"

gingerbread boy: 17 3/4" x 1 1/8"

rooster: 14 3/4" x 1 1/8"

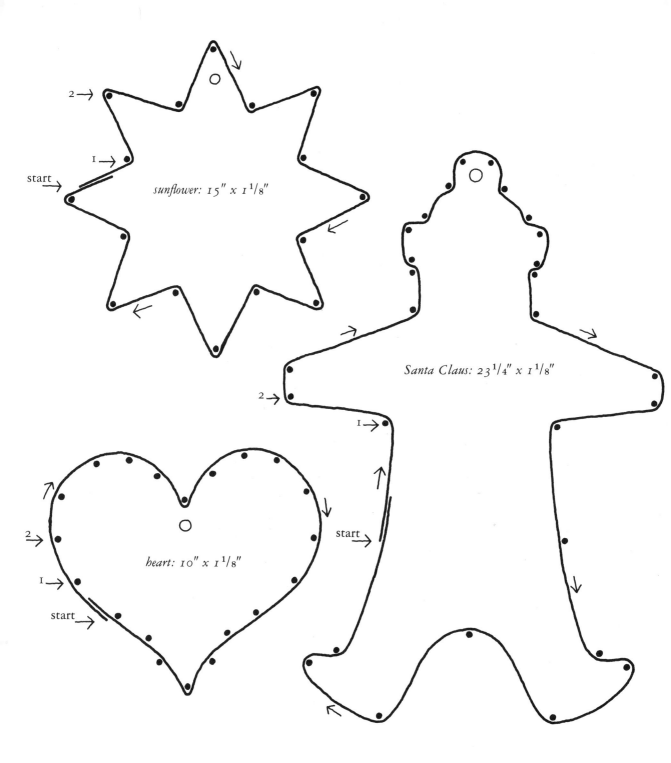

sunflower: 15" x 1 1/8"

start

2 →

1 →

Santa Claus: 23 1/4" x 1 1/8"

2 →

1 →

start →

heart: 10" x 1 1/8"

2 →

1 →

start →

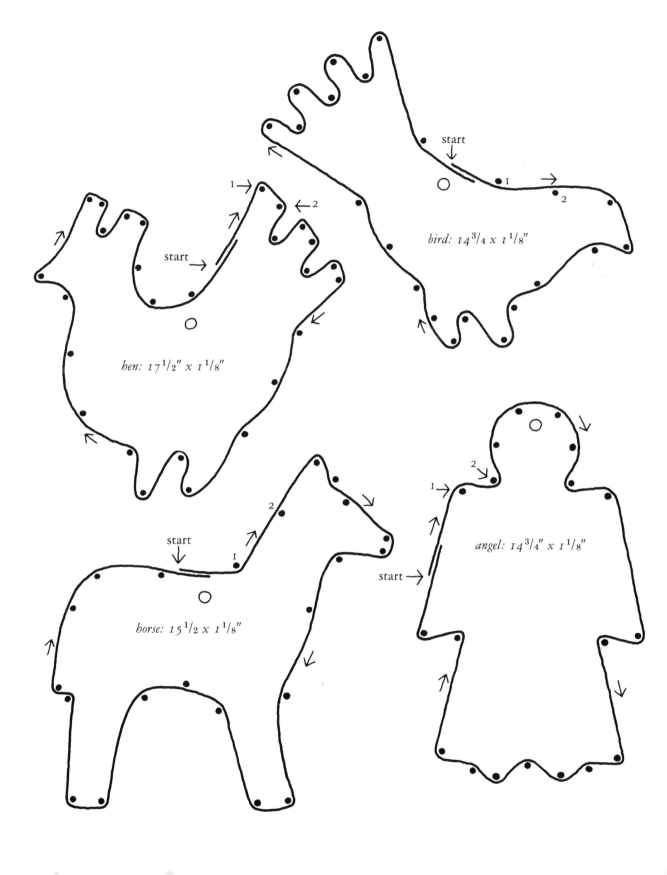

bird: 14 3/4 x 1 1/8"

start
1
2

hen: 17 1/2" x 1 1/8"

start
1
2

horse: 15 1/2 x 1 1/8"

start
1
2

angel: 14 3/4" x 1 1/8"

start
1
2

|←——————————————— 30″ ———————————————→|

star: $11^1/4''$ x $1^1/8''$	gingerbread boy: $17^3/4''$ x $1^1/8''$	
horse: $15^1/2''$ x $1^1/8''$	heart: $10''$ x $1^1/8''$	
rooster: $14^3/4''$ x $1^1/8''$	sunflower: $15''$ x $1^1/8''$	
bird: $14^3/4''$ x $1^1/8''$	angel: $15''$ x $1^1/8''$	
hen: $17^1/2''$ x $1^1/8''$	tree: $10''$ x $1^1/8''$	
Santa Claus: $23^1/2''$ x $1^1/8''$		
circle: $7^1/2''$ x $1^1/8''$	←⊢hole: $3^1/2''$ x $1^1/8''$	

9″

*Layout of the strips
for the cookie cutters*

sign are shown on the diagram. If you plan to make all twelve cutters and the "doughnut hole" cutter, described later in the chapter, follow the layout shown. All the cookie cutters are to be made from straight strips $1^1/8$ inches wide. Lay out the strips touching each other, so as to conserve metal and so that one cut can serve for the sides and ends of each of two strips.

Now place the ruler on one of the lines, and using the point of the awl as you would a pencil, go over the pen line. Be careful not to smudge the ink—which is not very black or permanent. Scratch a clear accurate line into the metal going over it more than once if necessary, to make a permanent cutting guideline that you can see easily. Go over all the pen lines in the same way.

If you have a little extra aluminum, scratch a straight line on it and practice cutting with the tin snips until you can follow the line very

128

accurately. Tin snips are heavy, and if you have never used them before, they will seem awkward at first, but do *not* use scissors for cutting metal as it will ruin the blades. Now cut out carefully the aluminum strips for your cookie cutters. If they curl up, straighten and flatten them with your fingers afterwards.

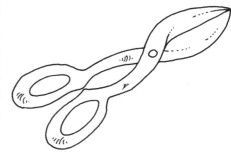

Folding the Edges of the Aluminum Strips

Next you must bend over and flatten one long edge of each metal strip, so as to make a finished edge at the top of the cookie cutter. This will strengthen the final piece and will also provide a safe edge against which you can press your fingers to cut through the rolled-out cookie dough. To make this folded edge, mark first with the pen, then scratch the line with the awl, a guideline 3/8 inch in from one of the long edges of the strip.

For the edge-bending operation a vise with strong jaws is essential. Wind up the handle of the vise until there is only a small slot between the two jaws. Starting at one end of the aluminum strip, slip the narrow marked edge between the jaws of the vise so that the scratched line is exactly even with the top of one jaw. The slightly wider 3/4-inch edge of the metal strip should stick up above the vise. You will need very direct light on your work in order to be

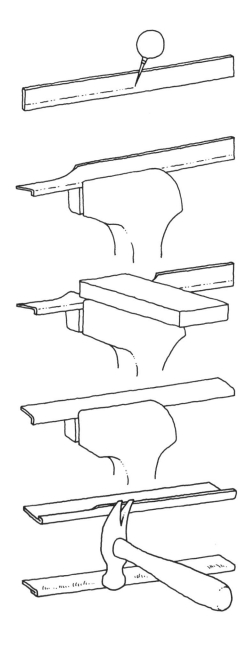

able to see the scratched guideline, and it is important to clamp the metal absolutely *straight* in the vise. Tighten the vise so that it grips the piece of aluminum firmly.

Now hold the small piece of $3/4$- by 2- by 6-inch wood board so that its 2-inch side is against the aluminum sticking up in the vise. Press the wood against the metal, pushing away from yourself with your thumbs until the aluminum is bent down to form a square bend of 45 degrees. Loosen the jaws of the vise a little, move the strip along past the small curve that will have developed in the edge, clamp carefully on the scratched guideline, and bend again in the same way. Continue moving the strip and bending the edge until you come to the end of the strip. Now go back and clamp the aluminum in the same way again and bend it wherever there is a curve or bump, until you have a true straight edge along the whole piece.

Take the aluminum out of the vise and lay it near the edge of your worktable, with the bent edge turned up and nearest you. Press that edge down, pushing away from yourself with your thumbs, moving along slowly and pressing an inch or two at a time, repeating the process until you have pressed the folded edge down as flat as possible. Turn the strip over with the folded edge down, and tap along that edge very gently with the hammer, working slowly until the whole piece is almost flat. If you hit the folded edge too hard, the metal will break and the strip will be spoiled, so work carefully. The strip is now ready to be shaped into a cookie cutter.

Forming the Cookie Cutter

The directions that follow are for the Christmas-tree design but you can use the same system to form any of the patterns. Cut out with the scissors a small piece of white paper the same size as the piece of tracing paper on which the Christmas-tree design is drawn. Put this under the tracing, so that you can see the pen lines more clearly. Tape the design and the white backing paper to the piece of plywood near the center of the board. Dump a few nails into a small lid or dish where they can be reached easily. Pound in the first nail on the dot marked 1 on the pattern. Drive it through the paper and into the board to a depth of about $1/2$ inch. An inch or so of the nail will be left sticking up. The nails must be driven firmly and straight because they are to serve as pegs around which the metal is to be bent. If you do not seem to be able to sock the nail in straight, practice a little on another scrap of wood.

After the first nail, do not pound in the nail marked 2—or any others—until you have started shaping the aluminum. The procedure to follow is to bend the metal into position first, directing the strip as indicated by the small arrows on the diagram. Pound in the next nail only *after* you have shaped the metal strip into position ready for bending around the nail.

To start, hold the metal strip standing on edge with the folded edge up and turned to the inside of the shape you are forming. Be sure that the folded edge is not on the outside of the cutter, because in that position the aluminum strongly resists bending. The unfolded or cutting edge must be down. Place one end of the metal strip on the part of the pattern marked "start." The edge should be exactly on the pattern line. Direct the long end of the strip upward toward nail 1 at the top of the tree. Press the aluminum tightly against the nail with your fingers and "wrap" it around the nail, making a sharp bend until the strip matches the line of the pattern. Continue with the shaping until you reach nail 2—which is not there yet! Then releasing the strip temporarily so that both your hands are free, drive in nail 2 at the bottom right-hand corner of the tree, exactly on the point marked. Holding the aluminum strip outside the nail, put the edge on the pattern line, and bend the strip around nail 2 to form a sharp, clean corner. Continue shaping until you reach nail 3.

If you look one step ahead to the next bend, you will see that when you reverse the direction of the bend (as around nail 3), you must not drive the nail into the board until the metal is placed in the proper position for the next bend

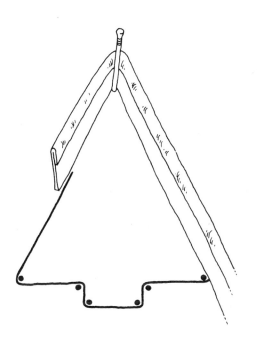

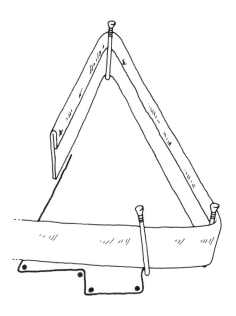

you are to make. Although the nails must always come on the *inside* of each bend they are sometimes on the outside of the strip. Placing the nails accurately is very important, for that is what gives a true shape to the cookie cutter and keeps it looking exactly like the pattern. An out-of-place nail will make a crooked Christmas tree or a star that is out of shape. And, of course, it will cut funny-looking cookies. So make sure that the free end of the metal strip is put in place just inside the spot where the third nail will go. Drive in nail 3 so that the bend around it will keep the aluminum strip going in the right direction. Now hold the metal tightly against both nails 2 and 3 with one hand, and make the third sharp bend with the other hand.

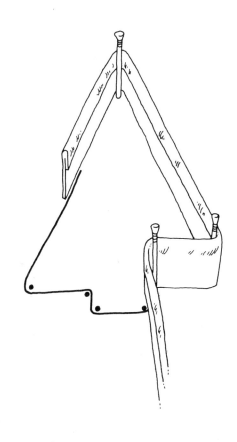

133

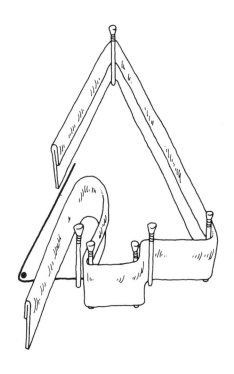

Direct the metal slightly *outside* the line this time, because you are going to change direction again. Drive in nail 4 and bend the metal around it. Follow the line toward nail 5, put in the nail, and bend the metal around it.

Now you will discover that you have a problem. And the same problem will come up at this point in making all the cookie cutters. As you near the end of the design and try to make the last bend or two, you will find that you do not have enough room to proceed because the free end of the aluminum bumps into the start of the strip. It will seem that there is no way to make that next bend!

There are two ways of solving this problem. The first and best way is to put the aluminum into position to make the bend around nail 6 by pushing up a temporary loop in the strip as if it were a piece of soft ribbon. The loop, or bend, will allow you to hold that strip in position, so that you can drive nail 6 inside that temporary loop. Make the sharp bend around the nail, straighten out the temporary loop by pressing it out with your fingers, and go on to the last corner where you can now drive in nail 7 and make the last sharp bend outside it. Where the two ends of the metal join there will be an overlap of about $1/2$ inch. It is the extreme flexibility of the aluminum that makes it possible to bend and unbend it without damage, and you can make use of this characteristic in finishing all your patterns.

The other way to solve the problem is to pull out nail 1 (read the instructions given below first) and temporarily bend up or lift the top half of the tree out of your way. Later, when the cutter is free, you can reshape it with your fingers to fit the drawing again. This procedure of pulling out the first nail will not work well with complicated and curvy designs that are difficult to reshape, but it can be used with the Christmas tree and the star, and even with the sunflower.

Pulling Out the Nails

The aluminum cookie cutter is now temporarily locked in place by the nails you drove into the plywood, and freeing it by pulling out the nails is not as easy as you might expect, even if you have used the nail-pulling claw of a hammer before. This time the bent aluminum is in the way, and you must be careful not to damage the finished cutter.

The trick is to use the small piece of wood board as a sort of platform to support the head of the hammer as you pull. If you put the piece of wood flat on the plywood to which the cutter is attached, the surface of the small piece of board will be almost level with the nailheads. Hold one end of the small piece of board against the cutter and next to a nail. Slip the two halves of the hammer claw over the nailhead, rock the

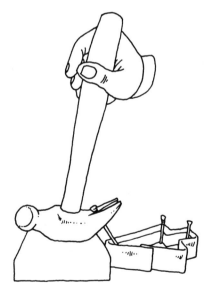

hammer head on the small board by pulling back on the hammer handle, and the nail will come out. If some nails cannot be reached to be gripped by the claw of the hammer, leave them until last. Then, if the cutter still is not free, pull out the confining nails with the bull-nose pliers. The cookie cutter usually will come free even when a few nails are still in place.

Putting the Cookie Cutter Together

Pull the remaining nails out of the board—if there are any—but leave the tracing in place. Now stand the cookie cutter on the tracing again to see if the cutting edge exactly matches the pattern line. The top folded edge may have a few bumps in it, but this does not really matter; if you like, you can straighten them with a squeeze of the needle-nose pliers. On the other hand, the single edge, which is the cutting edge, must be shaped perfectly. Use your fingers or the pliers with care to form it accurately, bending the whole cutter if necessary, so that it will finally stand level on the drawing with the two ends of the strip of metal overlapping and just touching evenly. This will take a bit of doing, but it is important to tug, twist, and push the aluminum gently until the cutter is exactly right. If there are stubborn little ripples in the metal of the longer straight sides of the cutter, put that area flat on the table if you can, and using the small piece of wooden dowel rod as if it were a tiny rolling pin, *roll* out the bumps. When the cutter is correctly shaped, you are ready to glue the overlapping ends together.

On a piece of wax paper or in a small lid or flat dish, which can never be used again for its original purpose, mix the contents of the two tubes of epoxy glue according to the directions printed on the tubes. The two different kinds of goo—one amber and one clear—have to be mixed together in equal parts before they become adhesive. A tiny squeeze from each tube will be plenty to fasten one seam. In fact, it would probably be better to finish several cookie cutters, and then glue them all at the same time, since very little epoxy is required for each.

Use one of the little tabs on the caps of the tubes to mix and apply the glue thinly to both ends of the overlap. Press the ends together, wrap a small scrap of plastic wrap around the joint, holding the ends of the metal exactly in place, and clamp them together over the plastic wrap with one of the spring-clip clothespins. Should any of the glue squish out, the thin plastic will prevent the clothespin from becoming permanently stuck to the cutter. Epoxy glue is incredibly strong, and it is the only kind of glue that will work on aluminum. It dries very slowly, so put the finished cutter with its clothespin clamp aside and do not touch it for twenty-four hours.

Immediately wipe any remaining glue out of the lid or dish, from the necks of the tubes, and from your hands, using a dry rag. When hard, the glue cannot be removed, but while soft, it can be wiped off with a rag. The solvents that will remove a big gob of still-soft epoxy glue are denatured (wood) alcohol or lacquer thinner. Next day, remove the clothespin and plastic, and your cookie cutter is finished.

By now you have probably figured out that you can make your own pattern for any shape of cookie cutter you want, if you keep the design simple. A useful cutter to add to your collection is a medium-sized, plain round shape about $2^1/8$ inches across. As shown on the diagram of the layout of strips, this can be made from a strip of aluminum $7^1/2$ inches long, with a folded edge like the others. It can be shaped by hand to match a circle drawn on paper with a compass, or it can be wrapped around a small jar or bottle and glued together like the other shapes.

Another circle cookie cutter that is fun to use is a very small one with which you can make a $3/4$-inch "doughnut hole" in the center of round or star- or flower-shaped cookies after they have been rolled out and cut. This requires a strip of aluminum $3^1/2$ inches long with a folded edge, and it can be formed by hand around a wooden stick or your own fingers. It will stay together without glue. The circle cutters are easy to make because they can be shaped without using the nails and board.

Before using any of the cutters you have made, swish them briskly in a pan of warm soapy water and rinse and dry them well. That magical glue will hold tight through any number of washings.

Making the Cookies

Now you are ready to become a *gëback* baker. The traditional Moravian cookies will be unlike any that your family and friends are apt to have seen before. It is best to use as decorations only things that were available in early times: sugar, raisins, currants, and nuts. For these particular cookies, avoid colored frosting and those stone-hard little silver balls called dragées. Both are modern and commercial-looking. Colored sugar is all right to use on the light cookies, and raisins, currants, and nuts will look well on the dark spice ones.

Here are some tips to make your baking easier. Use an electric mixer if you have one, though it is not essential. Use a canvas pastry cloth to cover the table on which you will spread out flour and roll out the dough. Use a rolling pin with a knitted cover and keep it well floured. Dip the cookie cutter in flour before *every* cut. Use two or more cookie sheets if you have them. Then you can let one sheet cool between batches. Decorate the cookies after they have been cut out and placed on the sheet but before baking. Make the holes for hanging the cookies with a wooden toothpick dipped in flour, moving it around in a small circle while the unbaked cookies are on the cookie sheet. Cool the baked cookies on a large smooth piece of clean brown paper backed with several layers of newspaper. A cake-cooling rack is not necessary; cookies dry flatter on paper.

Here are the recipes.

VANILLA SUGAR COOKIES

1 1/4 cups butter or margarine (at room temperature)

2 cups granulated white sugar

2 eggs (at room temperature)

1 teaspoon vanilla extract

1/2 cup milk (at room temperature)

4 1/2 cups flour (sift after measuring)

3 teaspoons baking powder

1 teaspoon baking soda

1 teaspoon fresh-grated nutmeg

1 teaspoon cream of tartar

1/2 teaspoon salt

Cream the butter or margarine in a large bowl. Continuing to cream the mixture, add the sugar a little at a time. Add the eggs one at a time, beating after each addition. Add the vanilla and the milk and beat well. Measure and sift the flour, baking powder, baking soda, nutmeg, cream of tartar, and salt into another large bowl. Mix well. Add the dry ingredients to the wet ingredients about 3 tablespoons at a time, beating after each addition. Beat only until well

140

mixed. Roll out the dough, cut out the cookies, place them on an ungreased cookie sheet, and add the decorations. Bake in a preheated 350-degree oven for about 11 minutes. Makes about 50 medium-size cookies.

MOLASSES SPICE COOKIES

1 cup butter or margarine (at room temperature)
1 cup dark brown sugar (packed)
1 cup dark molasses
1 egg (at room temperature)
4 1/4 cups flour (sift after measuring)
2 teaspoons baking powder

1 teaspoon baking soda
1 tablespoon ginger
1/4 teaspoon cloves (no more)
2 tablespoons cinnamon
1/2 teaspoon salt
few drops of vegetable oil

Cream the butter or margarine in a large bowl. Add the brown sugar and cream the mixture well. Add the molasses and the egg and beat well. Measure and sift the flour, baking powder, baking soda, ginger, cloves, cinnamon, and salt into another large bowl. Mix well. Add these dry ingredients to the wet ingredients about 3 tablespoons at a time, beating after each addition. Grease the cookie sheets once with vegetable oil. Roll out the dough, cut out the cookies, place them on the cookie sheet, and add the decorations. Preheat oven and bake at 375 degrees for about 10 minutes. Makes 45 to 50 medium-size cookies.

You can make hangers for the cookies from any lightweight cord or heavy thread. Crochet cotton, obtainable at notions counters, is an ideal weight and comes in many colors. For each cookie, cut a piece of cord ten inches long and tie the ends together in a knot. Stick the center of the loop of the cord through the hole in a baked, cooled cookie, working from the front and using a toothpick as a poker. Draw the loop out the back far enough so that you can put the knotted end through it and pull up the hanger.

If you decorate the cookies too heavily, or if you decorate them carelessly, you will truly spoil them—not only their looks but their taste! They are delicately flavored with just the right amount of spices, sugar, and molasses, so their taste should not be changed. Work carefully and slowly with your decorations and be sure the cookies are made prettier by the additions.

Then, *"Fröhliche Weihnachten,"* as Moravians say to each other on December Twenty-fifth.

On Christmas Eve, the Czechs serve a huge, sumptuous dinner of many courses. No matter how many members of a large family are at the table, one chair is always left empty for the Christ child.

8
GARLANDS OF POPCORN AND CRANBERRIES

American Christmas-tree ornaments of the nineteenth century

The Pilgrims who landed at Plymouth Rock in 1620 were devoutly religious people. In England they had rebelled against the authority of the Established Church, and they abhorred what seemed to them to be its excessive rituals. In America, thousands of miles away from the repressions they had known, the Puritans took self-righteous exception to everything that had characterized the Church of England. They refused to recognize any of its feast days—especially Christmas. In 1659 the Massachusetts courts passed a law that forbade the observance of Christmas, and for the next twenty years anyone who so much as said Merry Christmas was fined fifteen shillings!

The early Puritans hated Christmas, and in her book *Customs and Fashions in Old New England,* Alice Morse Earle says that as time went

143

by the Puritans shunned the holiday more and more and it became "the bug that feared them all." Finally, over the years, these attitudes gradually changed and began to disappear in New England. But it was not until about the time of the American Revolution that most of such laws had been repealed or were simply ignored and Christmas began to be celebrated throughout the American colonies. So, except in the Anglican and Catholic colonies of the South and perhaps in German settlements, Christmas was not much celebrated in Colonial America.

Frontier communities were not a great distance from the coast—Deerfield, Massachusetts, for instance, founded in 1673, was a town on the border of the wilderness up to the time of the Revolution. The first part of the eighteenth century was a time when Americans led a simple existence and luxuries were not a part of life in most of New England.

The Christmas custom of setting up an evergreen tree indoors and decorating it with ornaments and candles was probably brought to America by settlers from Germany sometime late in the eighteenth century. But the tree was not an established part of the celebration of Christmas until more than two hundred years after the first colonists arrived. Even in England, where the holiday had been celebrated for many years, such things as Christmas trees and Christmas cards did not appear until about 1840. By that time seaport cities like New

York and Boston were receiving imported goods from around the world, and some Americans could decorate their trees at Christmastime with colorful ornaments from Germany, glass baubles from Bohemia, and gilt and colored papers from the Orient.

But many of the first American trees, especially in remote communities, were decorated with whatever was readily available: Indian pop-

A star-topped tree decorated with tiny lights, garlands of popcorn and cranberries, two kinds of paper chains, and candy-filled cornucopias.

corn, wild cranberries, cutout paper chains, little paper cornucopias to hold nuts and homemade candies, and perhaps a few wisps of cotton to imitate snow. The trees were lighted by small hand-dipped candles made of tallow.

You might like to re-create one of these "first" American Christmas trees, decorating it with the same kinds of ingenious, easily made ornaments that were put together by members of families who lived more than eight generations ago. Such a tree has a truly American tradition, and you can make a very pretty one with the simple, inexpensive objects described in this and the next two chapters. Of course, the tree will have the traditional silver paper Star of Bethlehem at the top, and a string of little electric lights to replace the candles of long ago. It would not be safe or sensible to try to reproduce those.

Strings of Popcorn

The first English settlers in America found that a strange, tall plant they had never seen before provided much of the staple food of the native American Indians. Corn, or maize as it was then known, quickly became important to the newcomers, too. Ground cornmeal and flour were used for cooking and baking, and there were many other ways of preparing the juicy, yellow kernels to make them edible, such as roasting, parching, and steaming them to make hominy. Soon it was discovered that the dried kernels of a rather stumpy variety of Indian maize could be heated until each grain burst open. These white flowerlike morsels, when salted and eaten hot, were a special kind of delicacy. Popcorn, as we call it, is still a unique and special food that we associate with festive occasions like fairs, circuses, parties, and Christmas.

Nobody knows for sure where or when the idea began, but it became the custom to string the white, baroque kernels of popcorn on thread and hang them on the branches of the Christmas tree as decoration. It is a simple matter to prepare these snowy-white garlands for your own evergreen tree, almost exactly as it was done long ago.

Materials and Tools
for the Strings of Popcorn

POPCORN, packaged in its own foil pan with a wire handle, all ready to heat. Or you can buy a container of dried popcorn to heat in your own popper.

DARNING NEEDLE with sharp point

SPOOL OF BUTTON OR CARPET THREAD, any color

SCISSORS

THIMBLE

WHITE CARDBOARD. You will need two $1/2$-inch squares for each string of popcorn.

Pop the corn according to directions on the package but do not butter or salt it. Freshly popped corn is crisp, and the kernels have a tendency to split as you push the needle through them. Popped corn that has stood an hour or two and has softened is much less apt to break and thus it is easier to string. The stringing procedure is so simple that almost no instructions are needed, but here are some tips. Cut a piece of the button or carpet thread to whatever length you want the decorative string of popcorn to be—three yards is a good length—and thread the needle with it. Pull only a few inches of thread through the eye. Take one stitch down and another up through the approximate center of one of the $1/2$-inch squares of cardboard; pull the thread through the card only until the needle is about six inches past the card. Remove the needle and tie the short end to the long section of thread, so that the knot is against the card. The cardboard will serve as a "stop" for the popcorn. Thread the needle again at the other end of the thread, pull about 18 inches through the eye, use the thimble and start stringing on the kernels of popped corn.

A brightly printed, antique paper cutout of a Santa Claus figure, pasted on a ginger cookie. You can cut out simple designs from Christmas cards and use each as a pattern to cut out a piece of rolled-out cookie dough. Bake the cookie, then paste on the design with flour-and-water paste.

Don't try to move each separate kernel all the way down the string; add on several pieces, then gently push the whole bunch along. When you are within about ten inches of the end of your thread, string on a second little cardboard square, fastening it with two stitches and a knot, as you did the first one; then snip off the end of the thread. The cardboard will keep the popcorn from coming unstrung and should be left in place on the finished string.

That's all there is to it, and all the members of your family can share the fun of this holiday project. Better keep nearby a bowl of popcorn that *has* been salted and buttered!

Strings and Circlets of Cranberries

Seventeenth-century settlers found shiny red cranberries growing wild all along the eastern coastal areas of America from Massachusetts as far south as the Carolina plantations. The small round berries grow on a low vinelike plant in marshy bogs close to the shore, and unlike most plants with edible berries, the fruit ripens very late in the fall.

American colonial cooks must have been delighted with the tart, juicy berries, which are still used today as the most colorful and flavorful part of many November and December meals. It was inevitable that the red color and

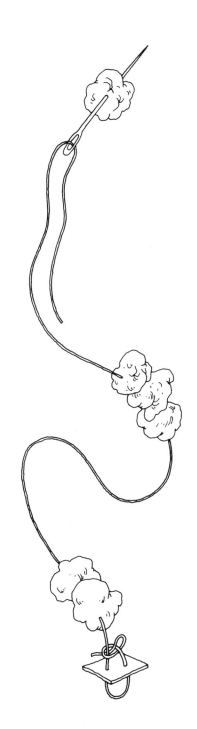

149

round shape of cranberries should suggest their use as a decorative string of ruby-colored beads for the Christmas tree.

Materials and Tools
for Cranberry Strings and Circlets

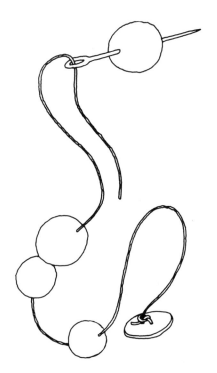

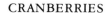

CRANBERRIES
CARPET OR BUTTON THREAD, any color
SCISSORS
DARNING NEEDLE, with sharp point
CARDBOARD or construction paper. You will need two red or green circles, $1/2$ inch in diameter, for each string of cranberries.
THIMBLE
FLORIST'S WIRE, small spool of #30
WIRE-CUTTING PLIERS or nippers
RULER

Sort the cranberries, discarding stems and any soft or small yellowish berries. Cranberries can easily be strung on a long piece of sturdy thread in the same way as popcorn. Use the small round circles of cardboard or construction paper (draw around the thimble to make them) to serve as "stops" at both ends of the thread. Using the thimble, push the needle straight through each berry, starting at the stem end.

If you are going to use popcorn strings on your Christmas tree, you may not want another kind of string, even though a garland of cranberries is different from one of popcorn. To give some variety to the shape of the ornaments on your tree, you can make another kind of decoration from cranberries—small circlets about the size of bracelets that can be slipped over the tips of Christmas tree branches.

To make a circlet use the wire cutters or nippers to cut a piece of florist's wire about 14 inches long and thread the darning needle with the wire. To keep the wire in the eye of the needle, bend down a 3-inch end of the wire at the needle eye and pinch the wires together. Using the wire as if it were thread, string on one berry; bend about two inches of the free end of the wire into a right angle to act as a stop for

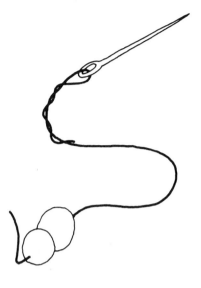

Circlets of cranberries

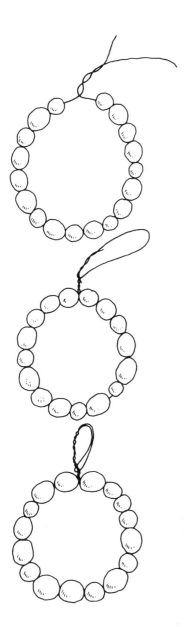

the first berry. When you have added enough
"beads" to fill up the wire to within about 6 or
7 inches from the needle (about fifteen or sixteen cranberries), straighten the wire, remove
the needle, and twist the two ends of the wire
together so as to form a continuous circle of berries. Then twist the remaining wire ends
together to make a small hanger-loop for the
circlet. Your Christmas tree will be more orderly looking if you make all the circlets about
the same size.

The photograph will give you ideas for variations on the circlet. One of the ornaments has a
little pine cone hung by a short wire inside the
circlet; one has a tinsel ribbon bow; and one was
made by stringing the berries on an 18-inch
piece of wire and then twisting the wire into a
figure-eight shape.

You may be surprised to see how effective
and bright these shiny red berries are when used
to ornament a dark green Christmas tree.

*In the Virginia colony in the seventeenth century the
Christmas celebration started with a big bang as all
the men in town shot off their muskets in a loud dawn
salute.*

152

9
PAPER CHAINS FOR THE CHRISTMAS TREE

*Colorful links
with tradition*

Ever since it was invented in China in A.D. 105, paper has been used in countless ways. Early European paper was usually made from a mixture of hemp and flax pulp. Each sheet was produced by hand to be used for the lettering of important documents and eventually for the printing of books. In 1798 a paper-making machine was invented in France, and this marked the beginning of the mills that rolled out a great many new kinds of paper. Today we are so accustomed to their variety that we hardly think of how different the world would be without paper!

In Colonial America, paper was very scarce; in the year 1765 the *Boston Gazette* carried this notice:

PAPER MILL. *The public are once more requested to save their linnen and cotton* RAGS

153

In the early nineteenth century when good rag paper was still scarce, decorated gilt and colored sheets were brought from the Orient to the New World by sailing ships. Printed French wallpapers and block-printed English "box papers" for lining trunks and hatboxes also began to be imported. At Christmastime larger sheets of these papers were saved to wrap special gifts, and smaller pieces were cut, folded, and made into ornaments. Every scrap of paper was used and reused. To decorate the Christmas tree, children formed link chains out of short strips of whatever kind of paper they could find. Today we have a dazzling wealth of colored and printed papers as well as shiny gold and silver foil to use if we wish to carry on the tradition.

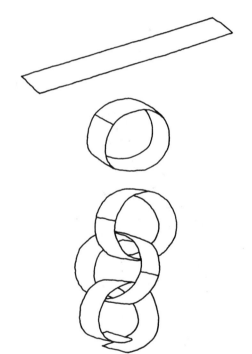

To make the simplest chain you need only paper and pencil, a ruler, scissors, and glue. Begin by cutting the paper into narrow strips of uniform width and length. Form one strip into a circle, overlap the ends about ¹/₂ inch, and glue them together. Put the next strip through that first link, form it into a circle as before, and glue the ends together. Continue this process so that each link is interlocked into the preceding link. Rubber cement is the best kind of glue, for it is quick drying. Apply the cement to both ends—but to opposite sides—of the strip, allow the cement to dry for a few seconds, then press the coated ends together. Other kinds of glue dry slowly, and the strips slither around in an annoying way before the glue dries enough to hold them.

Twenty-five strips cut $1/2$-inch wide and 5 inches long and cemented together with a $1/2$-inch overlap will make a chain one yard long. Or you can make a chain of the same length from twenty strips cut $3/4$-inch wide and $6^{1/2}$ inches long. On an average-sized Christmas tree the completed chain will hang more gracefully if it is about three or four yards in length, draped over several branches. A shorter chain will look too dinky.

You can use construction paper, gift-wrap paper, or tissue paper. Construction paper is rather stiff and will make a chain of firm, round links that will keep their circular shape if they are rolled with the grain of the paper. Light gift-wrap paper links will hang in an oval shape, and links of tissue paper will stretch to a much longer, narrow oval.

In Mexico, where it never rains in December, rows of laurel trees in the village square are decorated with long, airy tissue-paper chains made of links from strips cut about 2 inches wide and 12 inches long. The lazy oval links wave very prettily in the breeze.

But there is another, very ingenious way of making paper chains that look very attractive and quite different from the usual, simpler ones. These chains are formed of interlocking,

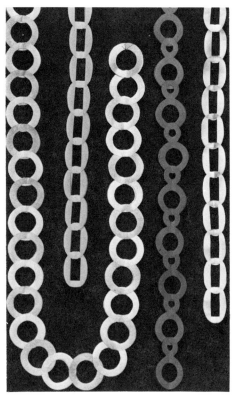

Swedish chains

folded, flat links which have been cut from a sturdy paper that is colored on both sides. The idea may have come from Germany or it may have originated in Scandinavia, since they are sometimes known as Swedish chains. The materials and tools required are simple, and no gluing is necessary. The method of cutting and folding the links is a little complicated but very clever, and results in an interesting-looking chain.

The diagrams show three different designs of paper links. Whichever one you decide to make will be traced on folded paper and cut out in such a way that the links can be connected to make a flexible, colorful chain. The photograph gives you a much better idea of how the finished chains look than do the patterns for the individual links. Two long chains will probably be enough for one Christmas tree. Their length, of course, will depend on the size of your tree and the way in which you hang them. The number of links required to make a yard of chain is given beside each pattern. The chain can be made of links of paper all the same color or of two or three alternating colors, as you choose. Try making a few experimental chains, each about six links long, in different patterns with different colors of paper to help you decide which will look best on your tree. This practice will also show you why the paper you use should be the same color on both sides—a little edge of the back is sure to show on each link.

Materials and Tools
for the Swedish Chains

COLORED PAPER. You can use either construction paper, which comes in sheets 9 by 12 or 18 by 24 inches, or Crescent drawing paper, which comes in sheets 22 by 32 inches and in about thirty colors. The Crescent paper, which can be bought in art-supply stores, is more expensive, but the colors are brighter, and the quality is better. Below is a chart that tells you how many links you can cut from standard-size sheets of paper. Use the chart to estimate how much paper you will need.

CLEAR ACETATE PLASTIC SHEET, about 7 by 10 inches, 3-point weight or heavier. This stiff sheet will protect the book when you are tracing patterns.

MASKING TAPE or transparent tape

TRANSPARENT TRACING PAPER, sheet about 7 by 10 inches

PENCILS, one soft (3B) and one hard (4H)—and one white pencil

STIFF WHITE PAPER, piece, about 3 by 5 inches. You can use any good quality card, heavy (2-ply) drawing paper, or bristol board.

RULER AND YARDSTICK. Both will be useful.

PENCIL COMPASS (optional)

SCISSORS, sharp-pointed, small

BALL-POINT PEN (optional)

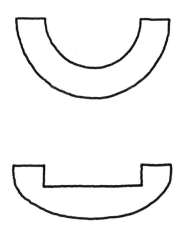

Patterns for three different designs of paper links: from top to bottom, Circles, Ovals, and Double Circles

157

Making the Links

Put the sheet of clear plastic over the patterns on the book page, then tape the tracing paper over the plastic. With the soft pencil, begin by carefully tracing one of the three designs—each of the diagrams represents *half* a link. The Circles design is the easiest to make.

Remove the tracing paper, turn it over, and blacken the traced lines on the back with the same soft pencil. Tape the tracing right side up again on the piece of stiff white card or bristol board, and redraw the lines firmly with the hard pencil in order to transfer the design to the stiff paper. Then, using a ruler for the straight lines and a compass (if you have it) for the curved ones, go over the lines on the stiff paper to make a more perfect pattern. No bumps are allowed, so start all over again if the lines are at all wiggly. Now cut out the little pattern very accurately with the scissors.

Here is a chart that tells the sizes of the small rectangles that must be cut out of the sheets of colored paper. Each rectangle will be folded and cut separately to make one link. Sheets of construction paper are 18 by 24 inches and sheets of Crescent paper are 22 by 32 inches.

PATTERN 1, Circles

Requires paper rectangles 2 by $3^5/_8$ inches.

Forty-eight links can be cut from a sheet of construction paper if the $3^5/_8$-inch dimension comes out of the 24-inch side. Twenty-six links can be cut from a sheet of Crescent paper if the 2-inch dimension comes out of the 32-inch side. Twenty-eight folded links will make a one-yard chain.

PATTERN 2, Ovals

Requires paper rectangles $1^1/_2$ by $3^5/_8$ inches. Sixty-six links can be cut from a sheet of construction paper if the $3^5/_8$-inch dimension comes out of the 24-inch side. One hundred and twenty-six links can be cut from a sheet of Crescent paper if the $1^1/_2$-inch dimension comes out of the 32-inch side. Twenty-four folded links will make a one-yard chain.

PATTERN 3, Double Circles

Requires paper rectangles $1^7/_8$ by 5 inches. Thirty-six links can be cut from a sheet of construction paper with the pattern placed in either direction on the sheet. Sixty-eight links can be cut from a sheet of Crescent paper if the $1^7/_8$-inch dimension comes out of the 32-inch side. Eighteen folded links make a one-yard chain.

For the design you are going to make, mea-

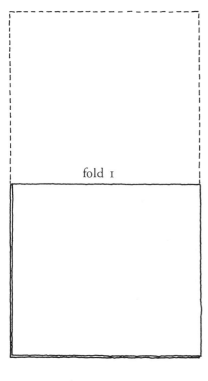

fold 1

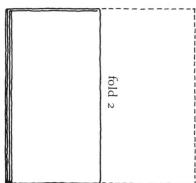

fold 2

sure off, draw lines (use the yardstick), and cut out the small rectangles. It is difficult to see a black pencil mark on a dark red, green, or blue paper, so draw the cutting lines on those colors with the white pencil. A rather soft, chalky material is used in a white pencil, so it must be sharpened often.

No matter which design you are going to use, each little colored paper rectangle must be folded twice. Fold the rectangle first crosswise, then lengthwise, as shown in the drawing.

The drawings opposite show how to place each cutout link pattern on its own-sized folded rectangle of paper. Hold the stiff paper pattern tightly in place and draw firmly around it with a sharp, soft lead pencil, white pencil, or ball-point pen—whichever makes the most clearly visible line on your paper. Hold the pencil or pen in a vertical position, so that you can make lines very close to the pattern. Note that each pattern is placed against the upper-left folded corner of the colored paper rectangle. If the pattern is placed in any other position, or upside down, your link will not come out right. Note also that no lines need to be drawn where the pattern touches a folded edge.

After you have drawn around the pattern, hold the four layers of folded paper together very firmly as you cut out the link, being sure not to cut through any folded edges, especially not the fold that must stay intact to form the hinge. That hinged area is marked on each pat-

160

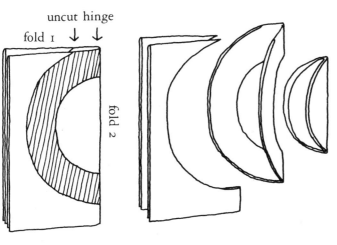

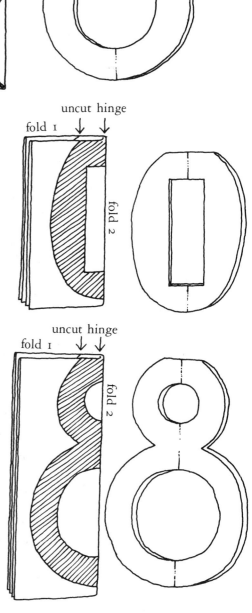

tern diagram. You may find it easier to hold the paper tightly if you cut out the smaller, inside openings of each link first, then cut around the outside. There are two good reasons for folding the paper twice to make the links: first, the links are double and hinged at one point—this is needed to put the chain together later—and it is only sensible to cut out the two matching halves together. Second, each link must have an opening in the center, and it is easier to make it by folding and cutting than by stabbing a hole later in the center of each piece to start the cut.

The procedure for making any link design is exactly the same. If your pattern becomes worn and scraggly, trace and cut out a fresh one.

161

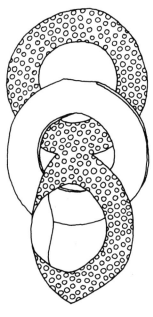

Once you have cut and joined two links, you will see that the method is really simple and ingenious, and also that it looks a little mysterious to someone who has not done the cutting. If the links are not drawn smoothly and cut out very accurately, your finished chain will not be neat and attractive like those made with care by your great, great, great, and so forth, grandmother!

Putting the Links Together

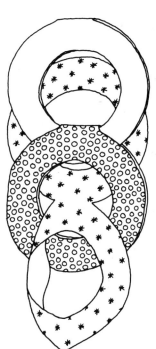

When you open out fold 2 of your cutout shape, you will have a two-layered, symmetrical hinged link (if you have done everything right!). To start putting the chain together, leave that first link closed along the hinge. Now unfold and open out *completely* another, identical cutout link. Gently and loosely roll together one half of the opened link until you can slip the rolled half through the hole in the first link, as shown in the drawing. Close the second link, placing its hinge opposite—across from—the hinge of the starting link. Continue adding links by opening, rolling, and inserting each succeeding link through the center opening of the closed link that preceded it. When you finish, you will have a flexible chain that can be draped gracefully and colorfully over the branches of your Christmas tree, along a mantelpiece, or over a window.

Now that you have learned the trick of putting the chain together, you can invent your own designs for the links and make an original, attractive chain. You will discover that if the links are too long or too thin and open, the chain will be floppy. So experiment with brown paper first to find the best size and shape for your links. You can be sure that nineteenth-century families had no books with patterns to trace for their chains! See what you can do with the idea.

A Word About
Gold and Silver Paper

Everybody loves gold and silver ornaments for Christmas—they seem to have a special, regal shine about them. It is almost impossible to buy paper that is metallic gold or silver on both sides, and white-backed paper is not very satisfactory for chain links. As we said before, a little edge of white is almost sure to show where

A nineteenth-century American Santa Claus figure, about four feet tall. Handcarved and painted, the wooden figure stood for many years in a New York City church. Its pack held programs, sermons, and notices of interest to the congregation. Photograph, courtesy of the Abby Aldrich Rockefeller Folk Art Collection, Colonial Williamsburg, Virginia.

163

the link has been cut and folded as the chain shifts in position. You can, however, make your own gold and silver paper by using spray paint, and a chain made of gold and silver links is very handsome on a Christmas tree. The paper will not have the high, reflective surface of foil, but it will have a nice, antique-looking metallic surface.

Buy two cans of aerosol paint, one labeled Bright Aluminum, one labeled Bright Gold. Cut two or more sheets of heavy brown wrapping paper to about 22 by 32 inches—the number of sheets you need depends on which pattern you are using for the links and how long you plan to make your chains. With the spring-clip clothespins hang the sheets about three feet apart on a clothesline outdoors, or in a very well-ventilated room indoors. Clip clothespin weights along the bottom edges of the sheets if they do not hang flat. Spread newspapers wherever necessary to protect areas that might be reached by the paint.

Spray both sides of the paper—one sheet silver and the other gold—with repeated light coats until the paper is evenly covered. Wait a few minutes between coats for the paint to dry. When the paper is completely dry, proceed with making the links and putting the chain together as described above. Some of the metallic paint may rub off on your fingers when you crease the paper, but this will not affect the gold and silver links, and your fingers are washable.

Hang your Swedish chain on the tree so that

the flat side of the links faces outward all around the tree. Let the chain fall in graceful swags from branch to branch to make an attractive and elegant decoration.

The first guest to enter a Scottish house on Christmas Day was expected to shout loudly, "First footing!" And he had to bring a gift of some sort, even if it was only a piece of wood for the fire. If he came without a gift, it meant a year of bad luck for the household. Because they were supposed to bring better luck to their friends than visiting women or girls, it was always the men and boys who went out "first footing" on Christmas morning.

The earliest-known dated Christmas card was drawn in 1842 by a sixteen-year-old English boy named William Maw Egley. The oldest-known American Christmas card was published by Richard H. Pease, an engraver, in 1851 in Albany, New York.

In the year 1904, a Danish postmaster published the first Christmas stamp, which he sold to raise money for charity. The country now prints a new Christmas stamp each year, and because they are so handsome, they are collected by people all over the world.

10
PAPER CORNUCOPIAS TO HANG ON THE TREE

*Bright cones filled
with sweets and gifts*

A cornucopia, or horn of plenty, has served for centuries as a symbol of abundance. Little hanging paper containers have been used as Christmas-tree decorations in Germany for many years and were probably brought to America by German colonists, along with the Christmas tree itself and a varied collection of paper ornaments.

You can make the small pointed cones from the same kind of colored paper used for the paper chains in Chapter 9. Filled with nuts, candies, or small gifts and hung on the Christmas tree, they will add color and a new shape to your collection of ornaments.

*Materials and Tools for the
Paper Cornucopias*

COLORED PAPER. You can use construction or
Crescent brand paper, fancy or striped gift-

*Paper cornucopias filled
with candies and tiny gifts*

wrap paper, colored shelf paper, or gold and silver foil gift-wrap paper. If the back of the paper is white, that is all right. As explained in Chapter 9, Crescent-brand drawing paper, which comes in many colors, can be bought in art-supply stores. It costs a little more than other paper, but the colors are brighter, and the quality of the paper is a little better.

SCRAP PAPER, in two different colors, for making experiments

CLEAR ACETATE PLASTIC SHEET, about 7 by 10 inches, 3-point weight or heavier. This stiff sheet will protect the book when you are tracing patterns.

TRANSPARENT TRACING PAPER, one sheet, about 7 by 10 inches

TRANSPARENT TAPE

RULER

PENCILS, one soft (3B) and one hard (4H)—and one white pencil if you intend to use dark paper

SCISSORS, sharp-pointed

AWL

COTTON CROCHET CORD, metallic cord, or ribbon, for hangers

RAZOR BLADE, single-edged

RUBBER CEMENT, small jar with its own brush (optional)

TISSUE PAPER (optional)

You can construct a traditional one-eared Christmas cornucopia by rolling up a single sheet of paper and fastening it with tape. Or you can vary its appearance in many ways, making a cone with a plain or scalloped edge, or by using two identical-sized cones, one inside the other, make a cornucopia with double ears or with a pointed or scalloped collar. A bright tissue-paper ruffle can be added to the top of a plain-edged double cone, and your choice of colors for all these variations is as wide as the rainbow.

Begin by experimenting with the scrap paper. You may have to try a few times before you master the trick of rolling a piece of paper neatly into a cone. It is also a good idea to practice attaching the hanger.

The traditional, pointed-ear cornucopia is easy to make. (See diagram.) You can make a small cornucopia for a small Christmas tree or a larger one for a tall tree. You can experiment in either size. For the larger cone, measure and mark with the ruler and pencil and cut out with the scissors a rectangle of paper $5\frac{1}{4}$ by $5\frac{3}{4}$ inches in size. On it draw a line $\frac{1}{2}$ inch from one of the

Patterns for the pointed-ear cornucopias

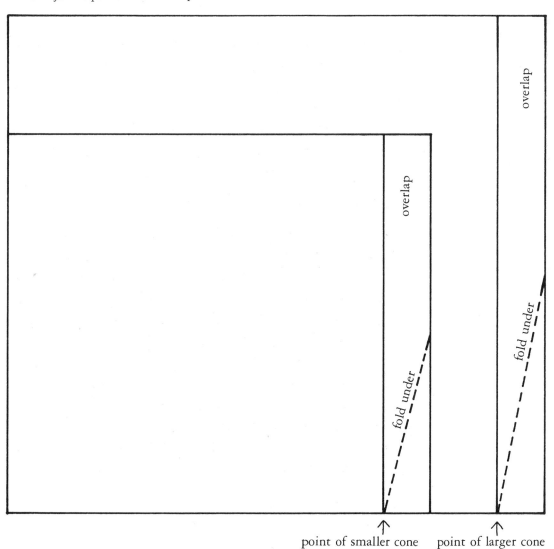

point of smaller cone   point of larger cone

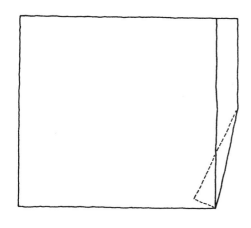

5¼-inch sides to indicate where the pasted overlap will come. For the smaller cone, use a rectangle 4 by 4½ inches, and draw a similar ½-inch overlap line on one of the 4-inch sides.

Start forming the cornucopia by folding the corner of one end of the cutout piece of paper *under,* as shown in the drawing. This fold is to reinforce the sharp point of the cone on the inside. Turn the paper over and press your thumbnail on the spot marked "point of the cone" on the drawing, which will now be to your left. Put the thumbnail of one hand on the marked point, pressing tightly against the table. With the other hand, starting at the upper left corner of the paper, roll up the cone. The folded section at the bottom should be inside the cone. Do not move the holding thumbnail at all, but roll the paper against it so as to form a sharp point. Don't worry about the size of the cone yet.

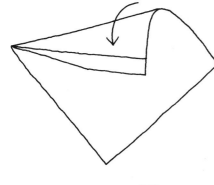

Now pick up the rolled cone, put the fingers of the "rolling-up" hand inside the top of the cone, and start unrolling or opening out the top more widely until the outer edge reaches and lines up with the overlap line. Keep a tight hold on the sharp point. If the point is not sharp, the top edges of the cone will not line up properly with each other. These edges can be aligned by pressing them together and slipping them up or down a little to change their positions, as you keep hold of the point of the cone with your other hand.

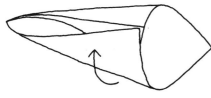

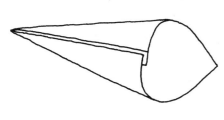

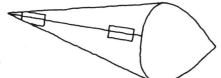

170

Two colored paper cutouts, about four inches long, used as Christmas tree ornaments about 1850. Photograph, courtesy of the Smithsonian Institution.

Tape the top of the cone together at the overlap line with transparent tape; then—also on the overlap line—add another tab of tape about an inch above the tightly rolled-up point. This will make a single-weight, one-eared cornucopia. To make a double-weight cone, repeat the rolling and taping procedure with another piece of paper exactly the same size as the first. Then slip one cone inside the other so that the two pointed ears are opposite each other and the seams are across from each other. Except for the

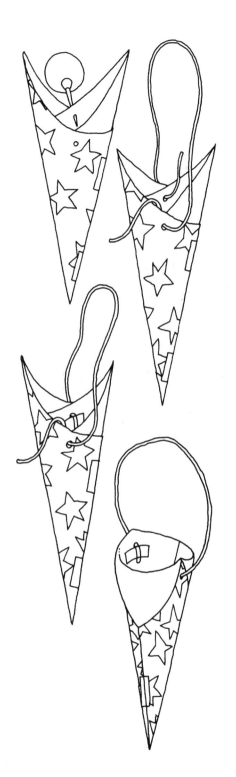

hanger cord, the paper cornucopia is now complete, and if you imagine it in brightly contrasting hues, with the outside and the lining of different colors, you can see that it will make a very pretty Christmas-tree ornament.

Now try attaching the cord hanger. Hold the two cones tightly together in place and, with the awl or the point of the scissors, punch two holes. One should be about $1/4$ inch below the edge at the low point of the cornucopia, as shown in the drawing. Make the other hole opposite the first one. Cut a piece of cord about ten inches long, and with the point of the pencil poke one end through one of the holes from the outside. Fasten about $1/2$ inch of that end of the cord to the inside of the cone with a tab of transparent tape. Poke the other end of the string through the opposite hole, again from the outside, and fasten it in the same way, adjusting the length of the hanger as you wish.

Now your cornucopia is finished, and the two points can be left sticking up just as they are, or they can be turned down. To do the latter, squash the cone together temporarily at the point where the two pieces of cord are, so that you can fold down the triangular points toward the outside of the cone, to make a sort of collar.

If you prefer, you can make the hanger from narrow Christmas ribbon instead of cord. Cut small horizontal slits in the cones with the razor blade and insert and attach the ends of the ribbon just as you did the cord. Or you can use

172

two pieces of ribbon and tie the free ends together to make a decorative bow in the center of the hanger.

You can make three variations of the pointed-ear cornucopia by using quarter circles instead of squares of paper. For these you will need to trace the patterns in the book, but first

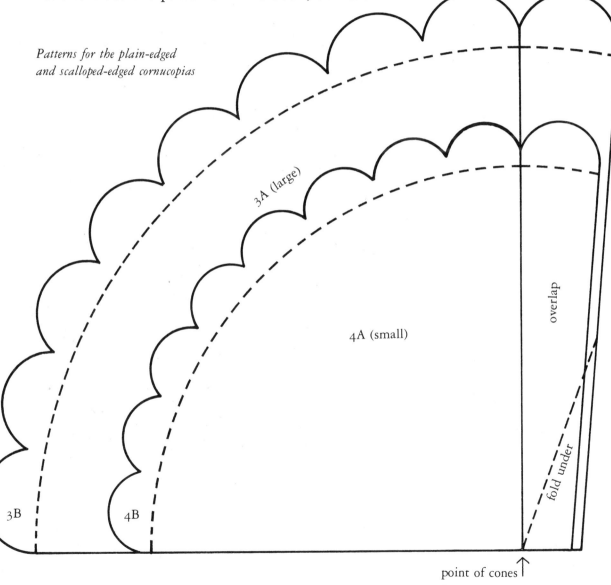

Patterns for the plain-edged and scalloped-edged cornucopias

3A (large)

4A (small)

3B

4B

overlap

fold under

point of cones

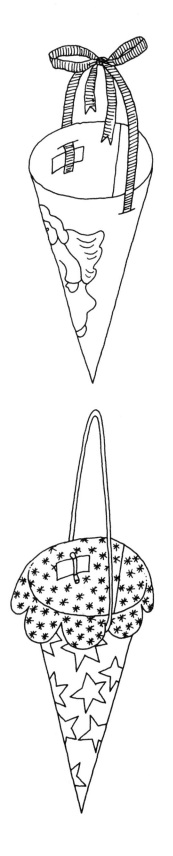

look at the diagram closely. One set, 3A and 4A, will make *plain-edged* cornucopias in two sizes that will look like ice-cream cones when finished. On the patterns, the rims of these cones are shown as dotted lines, which connect with the bottom and right-hand lines of the quarter circles to complete each piece to be traced and cut.

Superimposed on those two patterns, on the same diagram, are two sizes of *scalloped-edged* cornucopias, 3B and 4B. The scalloped lines connect with the bottom and right-hand lines of the quarter circles, to complete each of the two sizes of scalloped-edged cones.

You can hang either of the two kinds of cones as is—single-weight—on your Christmas tree. Or you can use the scalloped-edged cone as a liner for the straight-edged cones. By folding down the scalloped edge, you will get the effect of a fancy-edged collar. You can use different color combinations, making, for example, a cone that is gold on the outside with a scalloped silver collar and silver lining. Of course, you can't put the large cones (3A and 3B) together with the small ones (4A and 4B).

To trace the patterns of your choice, put the piece of transparent plastic over the book page, fasten the tracing paper to it with tape, and using the ruler and soft pencil, trace the outline and also the angular, dotted folding line and the overlap line for each piece. Remove the tracing paper, turn it over, and blacken the traced lines

174

on the back of the sheet with the soft pencil. Turn the tracing over again, lay it on the sheet of colored paper, and use the hard pencil to transfer the curved lines. Use the ruler as a guide to transfer the straight lines. Cut out the colored papers and form the cornucopias in the same way as before.

For a third kind of cornucopia, you can edge a double-weight, straight-topped cone with a frilly collar, made by pasting a tissue-paper ruffle around the top of the inner cone. The pasted area of the ruffle will be covered by the outer cone. To make this, cut out a rectangle, 3 by 9 inches, from either a single or double piece of tissue paper in the color of your choice. Then follow the drawings in Chapter 6 showing how to fold and cut ruffles for the piñata. With rubber cement attach the finished ruffle around the outer edge of the inside cone. Then slip on the outer cone and attach the hanger as before.

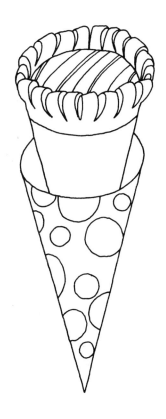

You can use any color combinations you like for your little paper cornucopias. Make them from any colored papers you may have on hand, including striped and shiny gold and silver gift-wrap papers and colored shelf paper. Since you need only small pieces of paper, you can salvage sections from attractive gift papers that have already been used to wrap packages.

If you don't like the looks of the little transparent tabs holding the outer cone together, you can, of course, turn the seam to the back of the tree where it won't show—or you can seal the

Painted wooden Christmas-tree ornaments from Germany, about 3 1/2 inches long. The dainty little angels are painted as carefully as if they were beautiful book illustrations. From the collection of Yvonne Forbath.

edges with rubber cement instead. Brush rubber cement on the two areas to be joined, allow each to dry, then press them together. If you want to decorate plain cornucopias, you can paste on small cutouts of flowers and stars or Christmas stickers. Fill the cornucopias with candies or tiny gifts wrapped in colored paper that will match or contrast with the colors of the cones. You had better make some extra "horns of plenty" to replace those your friends will want to take home with them.

176

Early on Christmas morning, farmers in Yugoslavia cut a huge log and bring it in to serve as the Yule log for the family. It is ceremoniously sprinkled with wine and corn and wrapped with decorative garlands, then lighted. When the log is burning brightly in the fireplace, a neighbor strikes it with a rod, and as the sparks fly, he recites a verse wishing the family a year of prosperity, good crops, and good luck.

In Greece at Christmastime two olive leaves are put on the coals of a fire, the leaves representing a young man and woman who are fond of each other. If the leaves curl toward each other, the pair are proved to be in love; if the leaves curl away from each other, the pair is not in love. If the leaves burn up without curling, the pair will be happily married.

Long ago at New Year's there was a Czech custom of cutting an apple in half, crosswise, to foretell the future. If the core was in the shape of a cross, bad luck would come to the person who had cut the fruit. If it was in the shape of a star, the person would have a whole year of good luck.

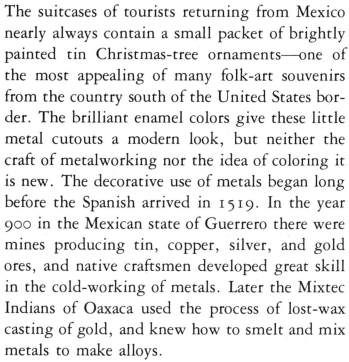

11
MEXICAN PAINTED TIN ORNAMENTS

*Shining decoraciónes
for Christmas*

The suitcases of tourists returning from Mexico nearly always contain a small packet of brightly painted tin Christmas-tree ornaments—one of the most appealing of many folk-art souvenirs from the country south of the United States border. The brilliant enamel colors give these little metal cutouts a modern look, but neither the craft of metalworking nor the idea of coloring it is new. The decorative use of metals began long before the Spanish arrived in 1519. In the year 900 in the Mexican state of Guerrero there were mines producing tin, copper, silver, and gold ores, and native craftsmen developed great skill in the cold-working of metals. Later the Mixtec Indians of Oaxaca used the process of lost-wax casting of gold, and knew how to smelt and mix metals to make alloys.

The Spanish conquerors came in search of gold to enrich their kingdom, and they were at first fooled by the appearance of a gold-colored metal used by the Indians, which was really a

Mexican tin ornaments

mixture of tin and copper. In the end, the Spanish found very little pure gold in Mexico. Hispanic designs had an influence on some colonial tinwork, but the painted Christmas ornaments of today are unmistakably Mexican in style. The designs are charming and simple, making use of Christian symbols, such as the Madonna and Child, as well as earlier ones—the sun of the Aztecs, for example.

Modern lightweight aluminum looks much like Mexican tin, and sheet aluminum, a shiny, soft material that is readily available, is easy to cut. It is familiar to almost everyone in the fabricated small trays that hold TV dinners and other frozen foods. It is so soft that you can cut it with scissors. If you then color the aluminum with a special kind of felt pen, you can reproduce very faithfully the painted Mexican ornaments. The bright shining shapes will flutter in the air on your Christmas tree or wherever they are hung in the house. The diagrams here show twelve actual-size patterns, eight large and four small designs taken directly from tin ornaments in the National Museum of Popular Arts and Crafts in Mexico City. The ornaments are very simple to make, and the cost is a lot less than a trip to Mexico!

Materials and Tools for the Ornaments

ALUMINUM. You can use either lightweight (32-gauge) tooling aluminum, which is sold in art supply stores, or "E-Z Foil"–brand cookie sheet, 13 by $17^{1}/_{2}$ inches, which can be bought two to a package in the housewares section of department or hardware stores. Two cookie sheets will make about twenty large and twenty or more small ornaments. *Note:* Kitchen foil is much too light to use, and both aluminum flashing and the tin from tin cans too heavy.

Madonna and Child, 4½ inches tall

Owl, 4½ inches tall

FELT PENS in six colors—red, yellow, blue, orange, green, and purple. "Sharpie"-brand pens, made by Sanford, are by far the best we have found. If you cannot find Sharpie brand, take a small piece of the aluminum you are going to use to a stationery or art-supply store and try out other kinds of so-called permanent felt pens to see which will color the metal in bright hues that will not rub off when dry. Some pens work fine on paper, but are very weak and pale or do not mark on metal at all.

CLEAR ACETATE PLASTIC SHEET, about 7 by 9 inches, 3-point weight or heavier. This stiff sheet will protect the book when you are tracing patterns.

TRANSPARENT TRACING PAPER, three or four sheets, about 8 by 10 inches

MASKING TAPE or transparent tape

PENCIL

RULER

SCISSORS. You will need two pairs of old but sturdy scissors—one large and one small.

GLOVES, old pair

FELT (preferably wool, not rayon) or two blotters or a piece of smooth, hard rubber matting. You will need a piece about 6 or 8 inches square to use for padding.

BALL-POINT PEN

EMBOSSING TOOLS, for indenting the metal. Any or all of these will be helpful: knitting needle, leather-tooling tool, orangewood stick, small, wooden clay modeling tools.

WOODEN DOWEL. You will need a piece about 8 or 10 inches long and $^{1}/_{2}$ inch in diameter, to use as a roller to flatten the metal.

TEASPOON

AWL, for punching holes

PAPER PUNCH

CORD, for hangers. You can use crochet cotton or Coats and Clark's Speed Cro-Sheen in red or green, or fine silver metallic cord.

Wise man, 4½ inches tall

Assemble your supplies and find a place to work where the light is good. It is best to start by tracing, indenting, cutting out, and coloring one of the simpler patterns, so that you can learn the procedure from start to finish. Then you will be able to go ahead with any or all of the designs shown. The method is not at all difficult, and after you've had some practice, you may want to invent some designs of your own. The large patterns are for use on a room-height Christmas tree, the small ones for a table tree or to tie on packages.

Begin with the fish, which is a design with a smooth outline that is easy to cut out. Put the sheet of clear plastic over the book page and tape a sheet of tracing paper to it so that the fish is near one corner of the paper. Trace all the lines of the design very slowly and accurately with the pencil. Trace also the little circle where the metal will be punched to insert the hanger cord. Pull up the tracing paper and with the scissors cut out the square or rectangle that contains the tracing of the fish.

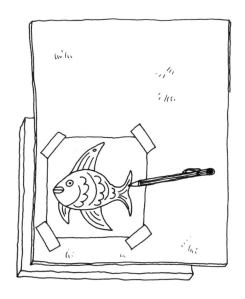

If you are going to use a piece of tooling aluminum, from an art-supply store, you are now ready to begin transferring the design to it. But if you are using an aluminum cookie sheet, put on the gloves and with the large scissors cut off the sides or turned-up edges of the tray; only the flat bottom surface is to be used. Bend the side strip down and out of the way as you cut around the edges, and discard it. Cut edges of aluminum are very sharp; be careful of your hands and always wear gloves when cutting, and especially when handling and disposing of scraps. Treat scrap trimmings as if they were slivers of glass—they are that sharp. Be sure that no tiny trimmings get into your clothes or shoes. Ouch!

To transfer the traced design to the metal, put the felt or other padding on the table, then put a corner of the sheet of aluminum on it. Tape the tracing of the fish near one corner of the aluminum. Use the ball-point pen to retrace all the lines of the design, bearing down just hard enough to transfer a visible indented line to the metal. Check your pen pressure by examining the aluminum after retracing a line or two. The lightly indented lines will serve two purposes: the outside lines will serve as guides for cutting out the fish, and the other curved and scalloped lines will be your guides for making more deeply indented decorative marks within the design. Don't press too hard or the pen point is apt to tear the paper, so that the tracing cannot be used again. This is not the time to try to do the final, more deeply embossed tooling of the decorative marks. You can do a more accurate job later when you are pressing directly on the metal. You will then be able to see better what you are doing and can follow the lightly transferred lines as if you were following a drawing.

When all the lines have been transferred to the aluminum, remove the tracing paper. Now, for practice, make a few deeply indented lines along the edge of the aluminum sheet, using the ball-point pen, knitting needle, leather tool, or the pointed end of the orangewood stick, to help you decide which works best for you. Always remember to use the felt or other padding under the metal when you are tooling it. You may find that the pen is the most satisfactory, easy-to-hold tool, and makes a clean, sharp line; the ink marks, if any, can be rubbed off with a tissue. Take a look at how the lines look on the back of your work. The ornaments are going to be colored on both sides, so there is really no right or wrong side, although the lines you *indent* on one side are *raised* lines on the other side.

Put on your gloves and with the large scissors cut around the design, staying about $^1/_4$ to $^1/_2$ inch away from the general outlines of the fish, so that you will have a smaller piece of metal to handle. If the aluminum curls up, roll over it lightly once on each side with the

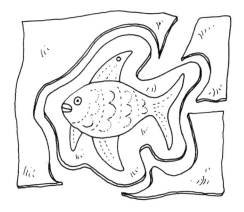

187

wooden dowel, using the dowel as you would a rolling pin. Do not *rub* the stick across the aluminum. Now if you have practiced tooling enough so that you can make a sharply marked line that will bring out all the details of the design, indent all the lines. Again, don't forget to use the felt or other backing pad. If the metal curls up, you can flatten it by rolling over it lightly on both sides with the wooden dowel, even after the lines have been tooled.

Cut out the fish, and since the tooled lines will show clearly on both sides, you can work from either side of the metal, changing sides as expedient. Cuts must always *meet* at the inner point of a V, for instance, so that scrap pieces flip out. Bending or pulling at pieces that are still barely attached will not work with metal, as it sometimes does with paper, so use the scissors very accurately. Now with the small scissors go back and snip off the tip of any sharp points in order to make handling the ornaments safer. If you don't remove the points, you may prick your fingers!

Lay the cutout on the table, and using the edge of the back of the spoon or the curved end of a smooth modeling tool, rub gently around the cut edges on both sides. This will smooth down the line left by the scissors along the cut edges. To make the hole for the hanger cord, lay the marked spot at the edge of your worktable and use the awl, pressing first from one side and then from the other. On the larger patterns you can use an ordinary squeeze-handled paper

188

punch, but it makes too large a hole for the small ornaments, and a larger hole than you really need for the hanger cord. Try making this size hole in a scrap or corner someplace and decide whether you like its looks or not.

Use the felt pens to color the ornaments in any way you like. Forget about the *real* colors of things, and use whatever wild combinations you want. The Mexicans use two or three colors on each ornament—usually in fairly large areas without much fine detail—and often the paint is rather blobby. Some designs have a lot of plain silver areas and others are solidly colored. The original Mexican fish, for instance, has a green eye, stripes of red and orange around the body, a blue tail, and one red, one yellow, and one orange fin. Some fish!

Experiment with the felt pens, working on the scraps of metal on which you made your tooling tests, and you will see how the bright transparent colors allow the metal to shine through. The felt pens are very simple and clean to use, and they have exactly the same effect as the transparent enamel paints used in Mexico. Color one side of the fish, and allow the ink to dry for about half an hour or more, then color the other side.

To make the hanger, cut a piece of cord about 8 inches long and tie the ends in a knot. Stick the center loop through the hole in the metal, put the knotted end through the loop, and pull the cord up tight.

Next, you might try making the Christmas-

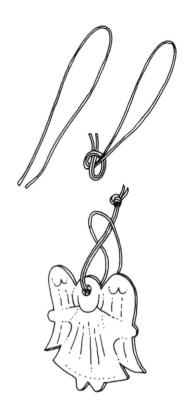

Late eighteenth-century,
Spanish-colonial, tin picture frame,
punched, tooled, and partly painted
in red and black. Photo, courtesy of the
Index of American Design,
National Gallery of Art.

tree design with the big flower in the center—a typically Mexican idea! You will see on this pattern—and on others—some lines of small dots. These are to be made in the aluminum by pressing down hard with the point of your tool, and they are an effective way to add sparkle to the ornament. When tracing dotted details like these, mark only the fine connecting lines on which the dots appear. The lines are sufficient to serve later as a guide for tooling the little beads as close together as you choose—you need not, in other words, follow the dots on the diagram exactly. When the dots run in a straight line—as on the robe of the wise man— use a ruler to guide you in tracing and transferring the guidelines. *All* straight pattern lines should always be traced along the edge of a ruler.

Here is a special note for anyone who decides to produce a lot of these charming Mexican ornaments and wants to cut down on the time required to color them by felt pen. There is a transparent enamel that can be used; it requires the use of a good small paintbrush for each color with turpentine as a solvent. The paints are called *Talens "Vercolor"* and can be bought at art-supply stores. They are transparent and are intended to be used to paint glass. A set of eight, very tiny cans of liquid paint costs about six dollars, but a little of the paint goes a long way.

On Christmas Eve in Lithuania the dinner table is covered with layers of straw to symbolize the humble manger of the Christ child in Bethlehem. The meal begins by all the members of the family sharing a single wafer, as a gesture of love, harmony, and goodwill.

If a young Russian girl wanted to know whether or not she would marry in the coming year, she performed a special test at Christmastime. Facing away from the entrance gate of her house, she gave a big kick so that her shoe flew into the air. If the shoe landed with the toe pointing toward the gate, she could expect no husband that year. If the shoe pointed in any other direction, that is where her husband would be coming from.

Many years ago in Germany, it was the custom to put a child's cradle near the altar of the church at Christmastime. In it was a doll representing the Christ child. As the congregation sang hymns praising Christ, the priest and altar boys performed a ritual called cradle rocking.

12
STRAW STARS AND ANGELS

*Two kinds of
celestial ornaments*

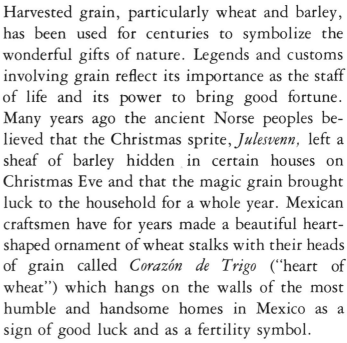

Harvested grain, particularly wheat and barley, has been used for centuries to symbolize the wonderful gifts of nature. Legends and customs involving grain reflect its importance as the staff of life and its power to bring good fortune. Many years ago the ancient Norse peoples believed that the Christmas sprite, *Julesvenn,* left a sheaf of barley hidden in certain houses on Christmas Eve and that the magic grain brought luck to the household for a whole year. Mexican craftsmen have for years made a beautiful heart-shaped ornament of wheat stalks with their heads of grain called *Corazón de Trigo* ("heart of wheat") which hangs on the walls of the most humble and handsome homes in Mexico as a sign of good luck and as a fertility symbol.

In many countries traditional small decorations and symbolic figures are made from the straw of ripened grain. In Norway, Sweden, Denmark, Finland, Germany, Poland, and

A Corazón de Trigo,
about 6 ½ inches wide, made in Mexico

Mexico, all sorts of little straw ornaments are fashioned for Christmas.

To make these small straw decorations, the ripened golden stems of wheat, oats, barley, rye, or rice are first dampened and then cut, bent, tied, sewn, or woven together to make stars, sunbursts, hearts, angels, birds, animals, and other decorative objects. In the pages that follow you will find directions for making two kinds of ornaments—a straw star, in several variations, and a small angel from Sweden.

You can buy natural-color wheat straw at a florist shop for a few cents per stalk. (Do not buy wheat that has been dyed.) After the seed heads have been cut off, a straight stem about 15 inches long will be left. If you live in or near the country, you can simply drive to a farm at harvesttime and ask the farmer to sell you some hand-cut straw. Or if you live in the city but have a country cousin, write and ask him to send you a mailing tube full of stems of straw; you can repay him by mailing back an envelope full of Christmas stars.

Wheat is probably the best and sturdiest straw to use, but the stems of almost any ripe grain or tall grass will do. Even the stems of grasses found growing along highways and in vacant city lots can be used. So, keep a sharp eye out for long ripened grass in your own

Swedish ornaments made from wheat straw.
The star is 3 inches wide, the angel 2 1/2 inches long.

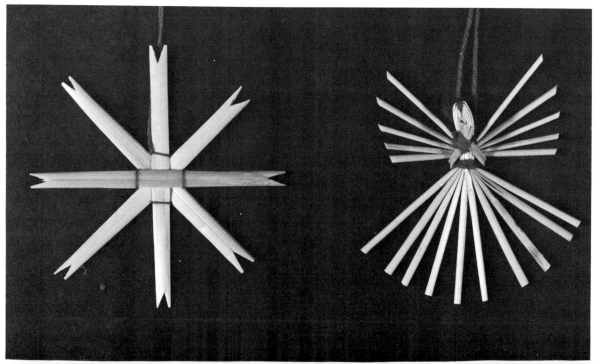

neighborhood. The stars and the angel shown in the photograph on page 198 are made from weedy grass that was cut down along the fence of a city playground. Start looking for grain or grasses in the late summer, or gather it whenever the harvest season comes in your area, and store a bundle of it in a dry place. It will keep until you are ready to start making your holiday decorations. In some areas, grain ripens in July, but in other places it is harvested in the fall of the year. In the far western United States, grain is planted in November and cut in June.

Green, immature grain and grasses and very old, dry, brittle stalks should not be used, nor should the baled straw fed to animals, which is usually too damaged and broken. Actually very little straw is needed to make these ornaments, but it must be ripe, and the stalks must be clean, unbroken, and still flexible. The leaves and seed heads should be discarded.

The airy, decorative stars are made from four or eight short pieces of straw, and the small angel requires only about ten or twelve short pieces, so you can see that from a handful of straw you can make a lot of Christmas ornaments. Two or more sections of the right length can sometimes be cut from a single long straw, or in the case of some kinds of grasses, from the straight stalk between the places where the leaves are attached. The distance between these leaf joints determines the length of the longest piece of straw you will be able to use.

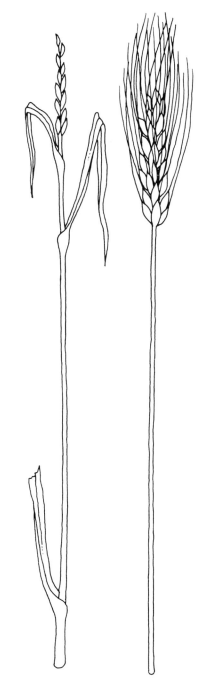

Weedy grass (left) and wheat straw

195

A Polish straw ornament.
From the United Nations Headquarters
Gift Center, New York City.

The shining, clean golden color of natural straw stands out clearly against the dark green branches of a Christmas tree, and the charming little decorations are so light that the slightest breath of air makes them turn a little.

Materials and Tools for the Straw Stars and Angels

STRAW, a handful
SCISSORS
RULER
PAPER TOWELS
THREAD, ordinary sewing weight in tan or pale
    yellow
THUMBTACK
CARDBOARD, two squares, about 5 by 5 inches
NEEDLE

The night before you plan to make the ornaments the straw must be trimmed and soaked in water. Cut off and discard any seed heads down to just below the first joint of the stem if the stem is jointed. Gently pull off any dry, clinging leaves by rolling the stem in your fingers to loosen them, then strip them off, and discard them. With the scissors cut up about twenty-four pieces of straw just above and just below any joints in the stem, so that you have straight hollow pieces that will vary in length according to the growth of the plant—usually the pieces will be about 8 inches in length.

196

Grain straws are usually very long and straight and without leaves. Discard any very slender sections from the tops of long straws.

Put the cut straw to soak in the kitchen sink or in a flat pan or baking dish, covering it with a small amount of water. Weight the straw down with a square dish or table knife, so that the water completely covers it, and leave it overnight. Since each straw is actually a tiny hollow tube, the water will moisten it on both the inside and the outside, and finally make the stalk so flexible it can be bent double and pinched together without breaking. Wetting the straw gives it almost complete flexibility, and it is surprisingly strong. This is the whole secret of strawcraft.

A German straw ornament.
From the United Nations Headquarters Gift Center, New York City.

Making the Straw Stars

Twelve hours later the straw will be thoroughly damp and ready for use. To make an eight-armed star, select four straws that are of about the same thickness. Measure and cut from them four pieces 3 inches long. Return any usable left-over pieces to the water and keep them wet with the rest of the straw until they are needed. Dry the four cut pieces of straw on a paper towel and tap or blow out any water left inside. *Warning:* straw left for two or three days in water may start to decay. If you don't plan to use all the straw right away, remove part of it

A Mexican star made from broomstraws fastened with fine copper wire

Four stars and an angel from ordinary weedy grass

from the water and let it dry in the air. Straw can always be wet again and used.

Cut a piece of thread about 15 inches long. Wrap or tie one end of it around the shank of a thumbtack and stick the tack firmly into a table or other secure surface. Fastening the thread in this way leaves both your hands free—one to hold the straw, and the other to weave the star together with thread. Otherwise you really need three hands or a helpful friend!

Now, between thumb and forefinger of your left hand, hold two straws at right angles to each other as shown in the drawing. Pinch them enough together in the center to flatten them. Slip another straw between your fingers on top of the first two straws, positioning it as shown. Press all three straws together tightly. Add a fourth straw on top of the third to make an evenly spaced eight-armed star.

Working about five inches away from the thumbtack, start fastening the star together. Wind the thread around the center of the "wheel" by pulling against the anchored end, passing the thread first over the topmost straw, then under the next one. Continue passing the thread over and under around the circle until you return to the beginning of the thread. Do not let go of the straws as you work; the thread will slip into place under your fingers and against the center of the star if pulled firmly each time. When you have gone around the circle, pull the thread up tight, hold it in place, and release the tacked-down end of the thread. Lay the star down flat on the table and make sure the threads are pulled up tightly enough to hold the straw in place, but not so tightly that they twist the star out of shape. Tie the thread together in a square knot, close to the straw, and snip off the thread with the scissors, leaving two ends about 3 inches long. They are to be tied together later to make a hanger loop.

Cut out a rectangle of paper towel about 4 by 8 inches and fold it around the star. Put one of the squares of cardboard on each side of the paper towel, and pressing the whole sandwich under very heavy books, two bricks, or some other heavy weight, leave it to dry. Pull the

199

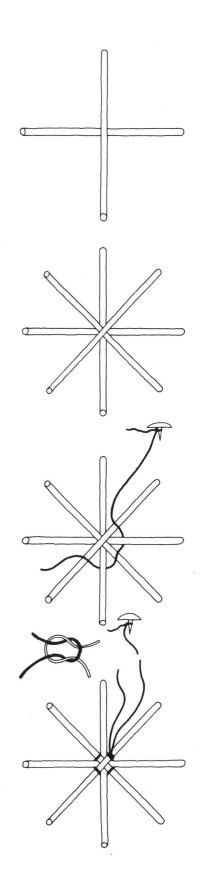

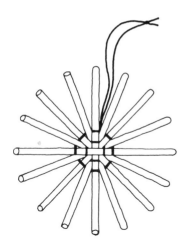

ends of the threads out to the side. It will take several hours for the straw to dry. Do not move the star until it is completely dry.

For a sixteen-armed star you simply make two identical eight-armed ones. Tie the first star tightly and clip off the ends of the thread short. Make another star and leave the ends of the thread about 15 inches long; use the threads to weave the two stars together and to make a hanger. Hold one star over the other with the arms in the position shown in the drawing and weave the two together just as you did the eight-armed star, going over and under each of the sixteen arms in exactly the same way. Tie the two ends of the thread together in a knot to make the hanger loop, and the star is finished.

As you can see in the illustrations, after the flattened stars have dried, the ends of the straws, if they are wide enough, may be carefully cut with scissors, either on a slant or in a fishtail-like V-shape. Or if you want, you can cut every other arm of the sixteen-arm star shorter than the rest. Whether the stars are the simple ones or the double ones, the arms must be carefully measured and cut to match. Otherwise the clean-cut effect becomes hodgepodge.

Making the Straw Angel

To make the straw angel you will need the same materials used in making the star, plus a sewing needle. The straw must be thick enough so that when you run a threaded needle crosswise through a group of stalks they will not split, and it must be moistened well so that it can be doubled over without breaking. Some grasses are too thin to be used for making the little figure.

To make the angel, you will need to cut five damp straws $5^1/_2$ inches long for the body and head. Cut six slightly thinner straws—be sure they match in thickness— $2^1/_2$ inches long for the wings and arms. These measurements will make a figure about $2^1/_2$ inches tall. You can make a taller angel by using longer pieces for the body and wings, but you may then need to add about two more straws to each group, so that the angel will not be too thin.

Lay the five longer straws close together with the ends even. With a pencil mark a line straight across the center of the group ($2^3/_4$ inches from the end). Thread the needle with an 18-inch-long thread and push it through the centers of the five straws at the spots marked. Pull the thread through and remove the needle. Wrap the two ends of the thread around the group of straws in opposite directions and slowly draw them together tight enough to make the pieces of straw flare out at the ends. Wrap the thread around twice again and tie it in a square knot. Clip off the thread, so the ends are about $3^1/_2$ inches long, and tie them together at the ends to make a hanger loop.

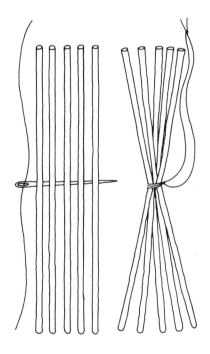

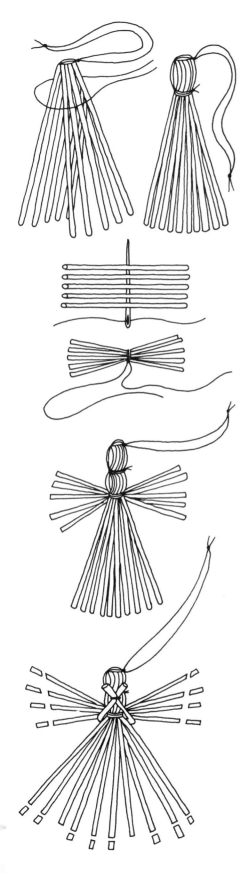

Bend the bundle of straws in half at the center tie and press the fold together. Wrap another length of thread completely around the doubled-over bunch very tightly several times about $1/2$ inch below the fold. This will form the head and complete the body.

For the wings, line up the shorter pieces of straw, mark the centers, and run a threaded needle through them, wrapping and tying the bunch tightly together with the thread as before. With the ends of the same thread, fasten the wings crosswise to the body about $1/4$ inch below the neck wrapping. Wind the thread around the body several times, pulling the thread up tight, and tie the ends together in a square knot at the back of the figure. Snip off the ends of thread.

To form the arms, bend the lowest straw of each wing group around to the front of the figure and tie them together by wrapping them firmly with thread about $1/4$ inch from the ends. Clip off the threads. Turn the two ends of the arms up a little to represent praying hands.

To finish the angel, trim the straws of the skirt, so that they form a neat curve, and trim the wings in a slant, as shown. The angel in the photograph on page 194 was made of wheat straw and has not been pressed at all. If you wish, you can press the skirt and wings with three separate weights. This will make the figure look a little less spindly, but be careful not to squash the head and hands.

202

That's all there is to the simple procedure of making the decorative little angel.

On Christmas Eve Norwegian families who live in the country put a bowl of porridge in the hayloft of the barn. The food is for the "barn elf," who is believed to have the power to bring good luck to the family during the coming year.

Or Christmas Eve in Danish households, dinner begins with a bowl of rice porridge sprinkled with cinnamon. One of the bowls contains a "magic almond," and the person who gets it will have good luck throughout the year.

On Christmas Eve, the Swiss have a way of telling what the weather will be for the coming year. An onion is cut in two and the halves are separated into twelve layers, representing the months of the year. Each little bowl-shaped piece is filled with salt and left overnight. The next morning, the layers are examined: those in which the salt is dry foretell which will be the dry months of the coming year; the other months will be wet.

13
A SWEDISH CHIP-CUCKOO

A perky ornament to perch on Christmas greens

Long ago in Scandinavia people believed that a cock with wondrous golden feathers roosted on top of a huge "world-tree." It was his duty to crow at dawn to awaken the gods in the dwelling place of the Norse deities.

This legend is undoubtedly the origin of the old Swedish Christmas custom of hanging a painted wooden bird or cock from the ceiling over the dining table. The "ceiling bird," although sometimes quite large, is light enough to move about in the air, and it is called by the affectionate names Christmas pigeon or chip-cuckoo. Many different sizes of ornamental birds and roosters are used in Sweden at Christmastime—to hang over the dinner table, dangle in doorways, decorate packages, or roost on evergreen sprigs and trees.

A present-day craftsman in Stockholm made the original of the small ornamental chip-cuckoos shown in the photograph. The material used was very thin white pine, cut out, glued together,

204

Two painted chip-cuckoos, made by the author

and painted with bright red and yellow watercolor. The little rooster perched on the evergreen branch on one twisted wire leg.

You can make a version of this chip-cuckoo using cardboard and a thin but stiff white paper—materials that can easily be cut with scissors. Your finished bird will look very much like the original when the various pieces are fitted and glued together and painted in bright colors. You can make it from easy-to-use diagrams, and the chip-cuckoo will be a delightful addition to the decorations of any Christmas tree, large or small.

Materials and Tools
for the Chip-Cuckoo

CARDBOARD, shirtboard weight, about 3 by 9 inches, for the bird's body

STIFF WHITE PAPER. You can use a good quality card, heavy (2-ply) drawing paper, or bristol board. You will need a piece 4 by 5 inches for the tail, and another piece 2 by 3 inches for the comb.

CLEAR ACETATE PLASTIC SHEET about 7 by 9 inches, 3-point weight or heavier. This stiff sheet will protect the book when you are tracing patterns.

MASKING TAPE or transparent tape

TRANSPARENT TRACING PAPER, sheet about 8 by 10 inches

PENCILS, one soft (3B) and one hard (4H)

RULER, plastic triangle, or a stiff, straight-edged card, to use when tracing and transferring patterns

SCISSORS, one pair, pointed and small

FINE SANDPAPER, No. 120 or 3/0

WIRE, 18- or 20-gauge, $5^1/_2$ inches long. Use either brass or galvanized steel wire. Copper wire is too soft.

WIRE-CUTTING PLIERS or nippers

STAPLER

WHITE GLUE, Elmer's, Sobo, Ad-A-Grip, or a similar type

CLAMPS. You will need four or five spring-clip clothespins or five or six big, strong paper clips to hold the pieces together while the glue dries.

POSTER PAINTS, a jar of red and a jar of yellow (and other colors if you wish)

PAINTBRUSH, size No. 2

CLEAR PLASTIC LACQUER, glossy or eggshell finish, in an aerosol can. Use Krylon, Testor's, or a similar type.

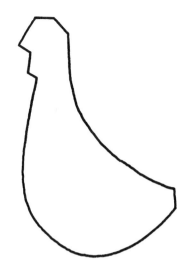

Assembling the Bird

The first thing to do is to trace the diagrams from the book. There are three: one for the body, one for the tailpieces, and one for the headpieces of the chip-cuckoo. Put the sheet of clear plastic over the book page, tape the tracing paper to it, and using the soft pencil, well sharpened, carefully trace the diagrams. Notice that the outlines of the pieces for the tail and the comb are straight. In order to make accurate tracings use the ruler, plastic triangle, or stiff card as you work, placing the guide exactly on the straight lines each time. Be sure your pencil is very sharp-pointed, too. These small pieces must be traced with great care and accuracy. When you have finished, remove the tracing paper, turn it over, and with the same soft pencil, blacken all the lines by scribbling over them on the back.

You must transfer to the cardboard the pattern for the body four times. Use the hard pen-

Patterns for the body (top),
the tailpieces (left),
and the headpieces, (right).

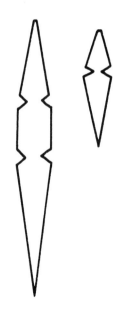

cil to redraw the lines, but do not press so hard that you tear the paper—remember you have to use the tracing four times! If necessary, pull up the tracing and blacken the lines on the back again. Work very slowly and press down accurately on the same lines each time. These four pieces must match each other exactly to make the four-layered, laminated body of the cock.

Now cut out the four identical pieces of cardboard, and holding the four cutouts together, trim off any rough edges until the pieces exactly match. Press the stack firmly together and rub the edges lightly with sandpaper to smooth the outlines.

Trace from the book the part of the diagram that shows the correct position of the wire-leg

Actual-size diagram
of the chip-cuckoo

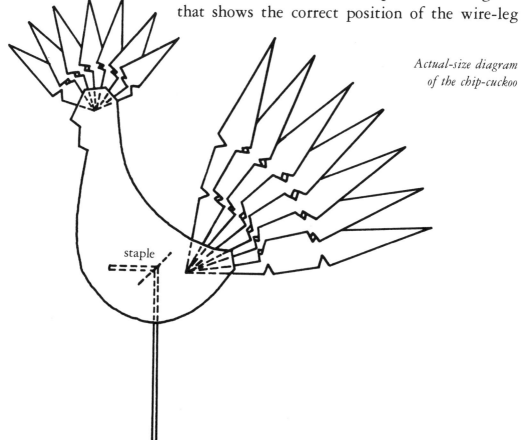

staple

attachment inside the body, and transfer that guideline to one of the cardboard cutouts. Cut a straight piece of wire $5\frac{1}{2}$ inches long. About $\frac{3}{8}$ inch from one end, bend the wire into a right angle. Tape the wire in place on the marked piece of cardboard, pressing it down well, and staple across the wire and through the tape in the position shown on the diagram. Press the staple down very firmly.

Glue the body pieces together in matching pairs with the wire on top of one pair. Spread the glue with your fingers and press the pieces together firmly. Do not glue the two pairs together yet. Put the two sets of pieces side by side and press them under a weight until the glue dries.

Transfer the tracings of the small diagrams for the comb and tail to the stiff white paper. Transfer each pattern seven times. Use the ruler or other straightedge to guide your pencil when redrawing the lines, reblackening the tracing paper on the back when necessary. Cut out the pieces; first cut the straight outer lines, then go back and snip out the small V-shaped notches. The notches are important, because they must fit together to help hold the fanned-out pieces in place, and they will not work properly unless the Vs are of uniform width and depth.

Now you are ready to arrange the sets of small cutout pieces to form the fanned-out tail section. Hold them against the diagram in the

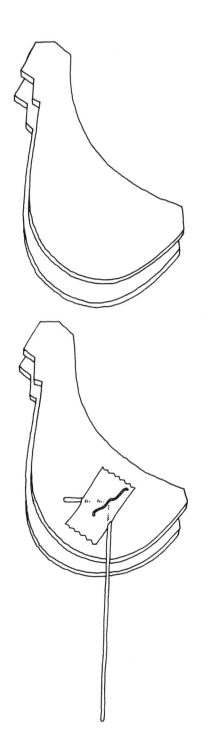

A St. Thomas' cross, 8 inches tall, made in Finland from three lengths of pine carefully "shaved" to form the delicate design. From the United Nations Headquarters Gift Center, New York City.

book to be sure the feathers are fanned out in the correct position. As you arrange the tailfeather pieces you need to perform a little trick. Put the pieces together as shown on the diagram. The notches should interlock, so that the more or less rectangular center sections of the tailpieces overlap from left to right, and the top and bottom sections overlap from right to left. By twisting each piece a little as you go along, you will soon get the knack of slipping the notches into place, and you will see how neatly they help to hold the feathers together. When the seven pieces are in position, put a narrow strip of tape across the group, just below the top of the feathers. Put another small triangle of tape along the bottom of the feathers. The tape at the top will eventually be removed.

Follow the same procedure, using the diagram in the book as a guide, to put together the seven small pieces that make up the cockscomb. Since there is no rectangular center section on the smaller feather pieces, put them together with the upper and lower ends interlocking in opposite directions. Secure this group temporarily with one very narrow strip of tape placed just below the top of the assembled cockscomb. Put a small triangle of tape on the bottom of the comb.

At last everything is ready so that the whole rooster can be sandwiched together with all his feathers in proud array. Remove the glued halves of the body from under their weight and sandpaper off any gobs of glue that have squeezed out along the edge. Lay the half of the body with the wire stapled to it on the table with the wire up. Press a tab of tape across the free end of the wire to hold it temporarily in place. Spread glue over the body and place the

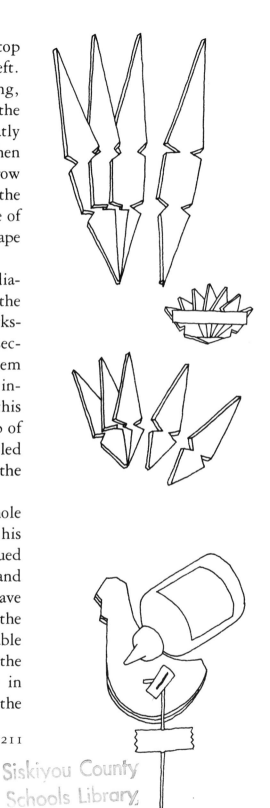

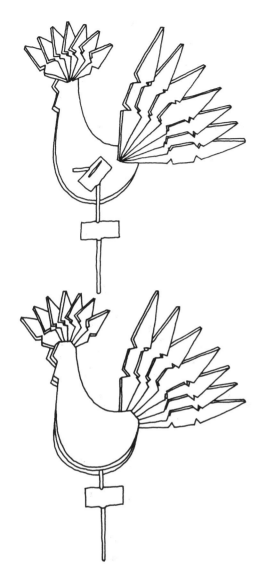

assembled comb and tail on it, using the diagram to help you in aiming them in the right direction. Add a dab of glue to the base of each assembly—comb and tail. Spread glue lightly on the other half of the body and put it on top of the first half; press the two layers together well with your fingers. Pull the tape off the free end of the wire, and using the spring-clip clothespins or big paper clips as clamps, put them around all the edges of your piece, especially where the tail, comb, and wire are inserted. Lay the assembled piece on the table and leave it there with the clamps in place for half an hour or more while the glue dries.

Painting the Bird

When the glue is dry, you are ready to paint. Carefully remove the strips of tape that are temporarily holding the comb and tail together. The little triangles of tape at the bases are now hidden between the two layers of the body. Sandpaper the edges of the body if there are any traces of glue showing. Stir each jar of poster paint until the paint is well mixed and about the consistency of thin cream. If the paint seems too thick, put some of it into a saucer and add a little water.

Hold the rooster by the wire leg. If you want your chip-cuckoo to look like the Swedish original, paint the body and tail yellow, and after they are dry, paint the comb and wattle red. (The wattle is that little hunk under the cock's throat, shown in the drawing.) Paint a big, round red eye. Paint both sides and also the edges of the cock carefully. If your cardboard is gray, it will probably need more than a single coat of paint. Stand the little painted ornament in a small drinking glass to dry. There is no reason why you shouldn't have a bright blue- or green-bodied rooster if you wish, or a many-colored flock if you decide to make more than one.

After the paint is completely dry, leave the bird standing upright in the glass and set it on a table covered with newspaper in a well-ventilated room. Cover any other objects on the table and the wall behind it with newspaper, too. Spray each side of the cock very quickly

An antique Swedish applestick
made of carved wood about the year 1700.
Used as a centerpiece on a
Christmas dinner table, it held
two tall candles and ten red apples,
which were struck on the pointed spindles.
It is called the ancestor of the
Swedish Christmas tree.
Photograph, courtesy of the National Gallery
of Stockholm and the Swedish Information Service.

with one light coat of lacquer. Wait three minutes, spray a second and then a third time, waiting between coats for the lacquer to dry each time. These light, almost invisible coats of lacquer will protect the paint from fingermarks and will seal the surface, so that the colors become permanent. Heavy spraying is not necessary, and it should be avoided.

Now your chip-cuckoo is ready to roost firmly and colorfully on the Christmas tree or wherever the end of his wire leg is wrapped around the tip of an evergreen branch.

On December thirteenth, families in Sweden celebrate St. Lucia's Day with a lovely early morning ceremony. The eldest daughter, representing the Queen of Light, wears a crown of lighted candles and a white gown. Singing the Sicilian song, "Santa Lucia," and carrying a tray of coffee and Lucia buns, she serves the other members of her family their breakfast in bed.

In old Germany a small, revolving construction known as a lightstock was used to decorate homes at Christmastime. Made up of four small shelves, one on top of the other, and lighted by candles, the lightstock was decorated with round cookies or wafers that represented the Host of the Eucharist.

14
A HOLIDAY FEAST FOR THE BIRDS

An outdoor Christmas tree

To most people, birds signify grace and joy, and it is not surprising that two charming old legends should link these small winged creatures to the Christmas story. According to an ancient French legend, a brown bird came to the manger in Bethlehem and stayed near the fire, flapping its wings to warm the Christ child. The heat of the fire colored the bird's feathers, and that is why the robin has a red breast.

In many rural provinces of France the tiny wren is much loved. It is sometimes called *poulette de Dieu,* or God's little hen, because it is supposed to have carried downy feathers and bits of soft moss to the manger to make a warm blanket for the Christ child.

Birds are enjoyed in all countries of the world and are usually welcomed whenever they appear. The idea of offering a special sort of Christmas hospitality to the small wild birds of winter may have originated in Denmark. In that

215

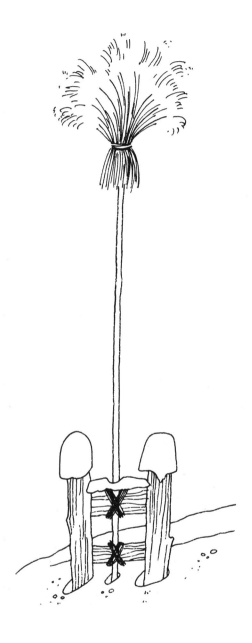

northern country it was the custom for farmers to tie a sheaf of ripe wheat or barley to the tip of a long pole and to set it up in the farmyard on Christmas Eve. Birds quickly discovered the feast and had a fine breakfast of grain on Christmas morning. The soft twittering of birds and their lively fluttering about a feeder make a very cheerful winter picture.

You can provide a holiday treat for winter birds if you live in a neighborhood where there are small trees of any kind. The right foods hung on the tree will attract the chickadee, downy woodpecker, titmouse, nuthatch, cardinal, various warblers, and many other birds that spend the winter where you live. In wooded areas an occasional squirrel may come to the party, too.

The edible decorations for your outdoor tree can be put together so easily that the only materials and tools you need are some pine cones, a spool of No. 30 florist's wire, wire-cutting pliers or nippers, and a few kinds of food you can buy in any market. Read through the ideas that follow, and decide which of the things you would like to make.

You can begin by preparing treats of popcorn and cranberries. Small circlets of popcorn and cranberries that you can make according to the directions given in Chapter 8 are not only pretty to look at, but from a bird's point of view, they are decidedly edible. It will be a little easier for a bird to peck at these bright red and white treats if they are strung on small circlets of florist's wire—instead of long strings— and if each one is then very firmly attached with more wire to a tree branch.

Another special treat that you can provide requires almost no work—only a little planning before Christmas. Crab apples are highly favored by certain insect-eating birds, and the small red fruits can be bought in markets from September to November. Store the apples in a cool dry place in a paper—not a plastic—bag until it is

An outdoor Christmas tree for the birds with crab apples,
suet balls, pine cones coated with peanut butter, and
circlets of popcorn and cranberries

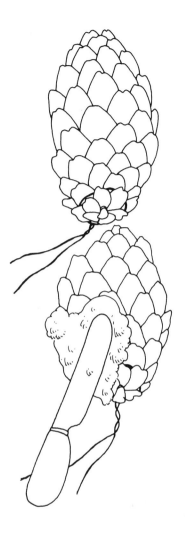

time to use them. To decorate the tree, hang the apples by the same florist's wire you used for the popcorn and cranberries. Twist the wire around the stem of the apples, or thread it through the fruit with a large needle, and attach the apples to the branches of the tree.

Most seed-eating and insect-eating birds—and all squirrels—seem to love peanut butter, and there is a special way to serve it to winged, nonsandwich-eating creatures. Before Christmas, search in your neighborhood for the largest and most widely open dried pine cones you can find. Collect a dozen or so. Wrap an 18-inch piece of florist's wire twice around each cone, under the first row of petals at the stem end of the cone. Pull the two ends of the wire out firmly in opposite directions. Using a butter spreader or table knife, spread the pine cone with peanut butter, pressing it into the open spaces of the cone until you make a small, almost smooth pyramid. Wrap the two ends of wire firmly around a branch so that the buttered cone sits on the top of the branch.

Certain insect-eating birds cannot survive the winter in good health without some substitute for their accustomed diet of bugs, which have gone into winter hibernation. Beef suet, or fat, is their favorite winter food, though seed-eating birds will have no part of it. You can very quickly make a number of small suet balls to hang on your tree for those who love fat. To avoid loud squabbles among greedy birds, make eight or ten suet balls.

218

Buy about twenty-five cents' worth of suet at the meat counter. Sometimes it comes in one big hunk, and sometimes it is in several smaller pieces. Chill the suet in the refrigerator for about two hours, so that it will be firm to handle. You will need florist's wire and wire-cutting pliers for the project. Wear rubber gloves to handle the suet if you don't like the idea of handling the greasy stuff. Use a sharp carving knife and cut up the suet into $2^{1}/_{2}$-inch cubes, or press smaller pieces into balls of about the same size. Unwind about 10 inches of wire from the spool and wrap the end of it around the first finger of your left hand several times. Then, holding the spool of wire in your right hand and the suet in your left hand, unwind the wire directly from the spool and wrap it around each suet chunk in all directions as if you were winding a ball of string. Continue to wind until the cube, or ball, is held firmly together, but no longer. When the suet is securely caged, snip off the wire, unwind the other end of the wire from your finger, and twist the two ends together. With the same wire, fasten the little suet balls very tightly to the *upper* sides of the tree branches—this gives the pecking bird a place to perch while he is eating. As the suet balls disappear, you can reuse the wire to make a new supply.

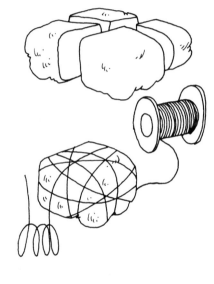

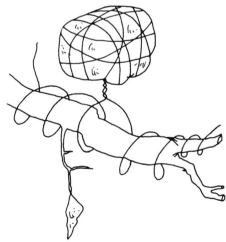

Mixed seeds are an important food for winter birds, but they present a real problem for use on a Christmas feeding tree. The feeder needs to be constructed, as all outdoor feeders are, so as to dispense food continuously and so that it can be refilled as the birds eat. If possible, set up or hang a well-designed commercial bird feeder in a place near your tree. If that can be arranged, and if you keep a big bag of birdseed on hand, then your buffet for winter birds will be complete. It is cheerful to watch the birds enjoying what you have provided.

Some experts say that once you have set up a feeding station, it is important to continue it through the winter months, because your bird visitors will very soon become dependent on finding their food in the same place until spring.

On December 26, St. Stephen's Day, Irish children go from house to house singing special songs and begging for gifts. The children carry a caged wren or a symbolic one made of straw and mounted on a stick. In several legends of unknown origin, the tiny wren is traditionally associated with the Holy Family in Bethlehem.

The longest way to say Merry Christmas is in Hungarian: "Kellemeskaracsonyi unnepeket kivanok!"

INDEX

226